A PARENT'S GUIDE TO SAVING FOR COLLEGE AND CAREER TRAINING WITH 529 PLANS

ROUTE
529

AVOID
DEBT & REGRET

PATRICIA A. ROBERTS

ISBN: 978-1-7357506-0-6

Library of Congress Control Number: 2020917864

Button House Publishing

Albany, NY

Printed in the United States of America

Cover design by Kostis Pavlou

TABLE OF CONTENTS

Start with your Destination in Mind: Embracing Your *Why* as You Begin Your Savings Journey

Getting off the Sidelines and on the Road: Recognizing that Now is the Time to Plan for Tomorrow

Know Before You Go: Examining Tax Benefits and Other Features that Make 529 a Preferred Route

Understanding the Terrain: Debunking the Most Common Myths Regarding 529 College Savings Plans

Going it Alone or Asking for Directions: Considering Direct-to-Consumer Versus Advisor-Sold College Savings Plans

Planning Your Trip and Developing Your Roadmap: Considering Your Time Horizon, Risk Tolerance, and Investment Objectives

DEDICATION

I dedicate this book in memory of my wonderful mom, Anne D. Roberts, who was responsible for teaching me my very first financial lessons, for instilling in me the value I place on education, and for encouraging me to follow my dreams.

Late at night, I recall peeking out from my bedroom door and seeing her sitting quietly at a table with a tiny light on, deep in concentration with a stack of bills, a note pad, pen and pencil, and her checkbook. As a solo head of household, she was attempting to balance a very tight budget to keep our family of five afloat. I knew it wasn't easy. She taught us how to save a little at a time for expenditures that didn't fit into our family's monthly budget. And when she encountered one of many bumps in the road, her resourcefulness, resilience, and unwavering faith in God prevailed. She left no stone unturned as she lovingly led the way through challenging situations. Through the examples she set, we learned the power of planning ahead for the future, coupling faith with action, working hard, having a grateful heart, and recognizing that our present circumstances need not define or limit us.

In terms of our formal education, despite multiple demands on her time, she always showed a sincere interest in our schoolwork, and was always available to help quiz us for upcoming exams, to be our audience for practice presentations, or to help support us in any way she could. Beyond this, she never missed a school or extracurricular event. Whether she was cheering my oldest brother on as he crossed the finish line in a Special Olympics track meet, watching my other brother play tennis, accompanying my elementary school class on a field trip, watching my sister on the field as part of our school's color guard, or attending one of our many performances or graduations through the years, she was 100% there for us with her undivided attention and admiration. For all she managed to accomplish with a very full plate of responsibilities, my siblings and I were as proud of her as she was of each of us. Her can-do spirit and love of family, along with her warmth, generosity, determination, and faith live on through each of her children, grandchildren, and great grandchildren. I wholeheartedly dedicate this book to her.

FOREWORD

As a college student, I appreciate the steps my parents took to save for my education, the opportunities I could pursue as a result, and the valuable lessons I learned by watching them plan ahead, a little at a time, for my future.

Knowing that both my mom (the author of this book) and dad were the first generation in their families to attend college, that they put themselves through college and graduate school while working multiple jobs, and that they spent many years repaying student loan debt after attaining their degrees (I was almost in high school by the time they finally paid off their student loans in full), I have a real appreciation for their commitment to save for me so that I could have an educational experience less financially stressful than they had.

As a result of having a 529 college savings account to rely on, I have been able to select both a university and a major that are a good fit for me, I have been able to focus on my studies without distraction, and I have been able to pursue volunteer opportunities, a study abroad program, and unpaid internships that align well with my interests. The account has given me options that I would not have otherwise had and has given my parents peace of mind.

From an early age, I learned that my parents were taking money out of each of their paychecks to save for college. The way they approached saving for me with small, consistent steps over many years helped me to learn about the value of breaking big goals into smaller, more manageable steps. I also learned how cutting back on things we really didn't need or avoiding expenses that were unnecessary could make a big difference. Spending less helped us save more. Through my family's experience of saving for college, I learned the value of planning ahead and setting priorities. I'm grateful for that.

While I don't recall exactly when I first realized that I had a 529 account set up for me, I remember knowing that I would definitely be going to college someday and that my parents and I had *something* that would help me get there. Now entering my final year of college, I owe many thanks to my mom and dad for the steps they took to get me where I am today.

I hope my mom's expertise will help your family achieve your educational goals. Good luck on your journey.

Ben DiFilippi

INTRODUCTION
WELCOME ABOARD!

Welcome aboard and congratulations. You've decided to learn about saving and investing for college and career training through 529 college savings plans—likely because you have someone in your life who will want to pursue further education after high school. You may be a parent, a parent-to-be, a grandparent, aunt or uncle, a teacher or guidance counselor, a trusted advisor, an employer, or family friend—or you may be someone who wants to start or continue education or career training for yourself. Like me, you may be someone who feels that higher education is one of the most direct paths to a rewarding life. Whoever you are and wherever you are in your journey, you've come to a great place to gather valuable information about preparing for higher education expenses with 529 college savings plans. It's never too early or too late to start, and I'm happy to have you travel with me as we explore this topic together.

By empowering you with information you need, my hope is that your family will be able to enjoy the many benefits that higher education can bring without the multi-generational burden that student loans can create. Here's some important data from The College Board:

- College education is linked to higher pay, upward mobility, improved health, greater civic involvement, and other valuable benefits.[1]

- Costs are on the rise. In fact, from academic year 1989–90 to academic year 2019–20 the average tuition and fees <u>tripled</u> at public four-year institutions and <u>more than doubled</u> at public two-year and private nonprofit four-year institutions, adjusting for inflation.[2]

As you can see, both the benefits and costs of post-secondary education are high.

To help you onto the path toward providing higher education for the future students in your life, I will not only provide you with information on 529 college savings plans but I will also provide you with specific steps to make the most of the time you have to save before the need to pay for higher education arrives. We'll explore your reasons for wanting to save and how keeping those in mind can provide motivation, how to stay on track once you've begun, how to spend less to save more, how to engage others in the savings process, and quite importantly, how you will be providing priceless financial education for your children through the steps you take to prepare for their higher learning. The planning and discipline you will

---

[1] *Education Pays 2019*, College Board Trends in Higher Education series.
[2] *Trends in College Pricing 2019*, College Board Trends in Higher Education series.

demonstrate are more valuable than anything they could learn in a classroom and will be carried with them throughout their life.

Why did I write this book?

I wrote it for a number of reasons.

Most importantly, I've been there. I've traveled the route upon which you are about to embark. I know it well. As a parent who saved a little at a time for my son's educational goals through 529 college savings plans, I know how good it feels to be prepared to pay for college now that the time is here. I also know the peace of mind and sense of accomplishment that comes with being prepared.

Additionally, as a financial services professional, I've worked closely with 529 college savings plans over the past 20 years and know exactly how they work, how easy they are to access, how versatile they are (they're not just for college!), and just how many very good and affordable options there are to choose from. I also know how useful they've been to the many families who have utilized them.

Also, as a first-generation college goer from a low-income family, I know how challenging it was to pay for college and pay back student loan debt over many years. I also know the many wonderful doors that higher education opened for me and how fortunate I was to be able to help my mom in many ways as a result. With this in mind, it saddens me to see so many students unable to pursue or complete higher education because of a lack of money, and I recognize the many benefits of education that they and their families will miss out on.

Beyond this, regarding those who do manage to pursue and complete degrees beyond high school, it troubles me to see so many graduates saddled with debt for years after and to witness the adverse impact this has on so many lives. I know that preparing in advance for the cost of higher education can make a meaningful difference for most families and can help reduce or eliminate the need to take out large student loans.

Further, it disappoints me to continue to see surveys reveal that nearly 65% of Americans are unfamiliar with 529 college savings plans. I am intent on raising awareness about the existence and usefulness of these plans, and how to open, fund, and use an account for many different educational purposes. My hope is that 529 plans become as familiar to families as 401(k) plans and other forms of investments.

And lastly, it breaks my heart to meet so many parents who tell me just how much they regret having not planned ahead for college costs or having not started sooner. They often share the heavy emotional and financial toll this has taken on their entire family. They almost always reveal that they wish they had known about an easy way to save when their children were younger.

For all of these reasons, and with many positive experiences in mind that have been shared with me by families who have used 529 college savings plans, I am determined to share what I know about these plans and to do so in an easy-to-understand way so you can be well-informed as you begin planning for one of the largest and most valuable investments your family will make.

With some knowledge about these plans, as well as commitment and planning on your part, you and your future student(s) do not have to wind up in significant educational debt. And you certainly don't need to go it alone. There is a different way to go and that's why I named this book **Route 529.** I hope you will enjoy accompanying me on this journey!

How does the book work?

- In addition to providing you with information you need about how 529 college savings plans work, I'll provide you with steps you can take to get started as well as strategies to choose from to help you stay on track.

- From time to time, I will also share with you what I call *Stories from the Road*—experiences that have been shared with me by other parents throughout the years, from which you can learn.

- At times, I will also give you **A** *Peek into My Journey* to share show how my personal experiences shaped my perspective.

- Lastly, I will wind up each chapter with a **Key Take-Away** section.

While I began sleeping better at night as soon as I established a 529 college savings plan account for my son when he was small, I could never have imagined how relieved I would feel when the time came to use the funds. As I look in the rear-view mirror, I am so grateful to have diligently saved and invested to be ready for this time.

It is my pleasure to be a guide for your journey and to help you find some relief by getting started. I hope you too will feel satisfied upon reaching your destination.

———

DISCLOSURE

A few points of clarification:

- While by name, 529 college savings plans include the word *college*, these plans are not just for college and are actually useful for far more forms of higher education than traditional college. They can, for example, be used for many technical and career-related programs.

- These plans are typically *investing* (versus *savings*) vehicles, although they are referred to as college savings plans. While some 529 college savings plans do contain FDIC-insured and other forms of savings options that minimize or eliminate risk and exposure to market volatility, more typically the options available through 529 college savings plans are investments. As such, they are subject to market fluctuations, meaning the value of the account may go down as well as up. Along with increased risk, however, comes the possibility of greater reward.

- I use the words *college*, *higher education*, *higher learning*, and *post-secondary education* interchangeably to describe a wide range of post-high school educational options. These include post-secondary trade and vocational schools, two-year and four-year colleges and universities, and post-graduate degree programs. 529 college savings plans can be used for many forms of education and career training that go well beyond what is traditionally thought of as college.

- I use the word *child* or *child(ren)* to refer to the future students in your life who will become your 529 college savings account *designated beneficiary,* or put more simply, *beneficiary.* This is the individual for whom you are saving or investing. I often use the word *parent* to refer to the adult (or *account owner*) who has established the account for the benefit of a future student. While you must be an adult to establish an account, the individual for whom you are investing can be of any age and need not be your child. The future student could be your child or grandchild, a niece or nephew, a loved one who is not related, a sibling, a spouse, or even yourself. There are no relationship requirements. You will, however, need to establish a separate 529 college savings account for each beneficiary. You will provide the name, date of birth, and social security (or individual taxpayer identification) number for each beneficiary when you open each separate account.

- The focus of this book is largely on **529 college savings plans** although the savings mindset and strategies I discuss can be applied to saving and investing with other vehicles. When I refer to *529 plans, 529 investment options,* your *529 account,* and make other references to 529, I am referring to 529 college savings plans. There are, however, two *other* types of 529 plans that have favorable tax and other benefits that are valuable for you to know about: **529 Prepaid Tuition** plans and **529A (ABLE)** plans. These are described in Chapter 12, *Considering Alternate Routes, A Look at Other Ways to Save.* While they are not covered in extensive detail, resources are provided for you to learn more about them. 529 Prepaid Tuition plans allow individuals to purchase future tuition at a pre-determined rate today. 529A or ABLE (Achieving a Better Life Experience) plans can be used for education and employment training but can also be used much more broadly for a wide range of disability-related expenses. ABLE plans can be extremely useful to eligible individuals with disabilities. You are not limited to one type of 529 plan—in fact, some families invest in multiple types of 529 plans at the same time. I'll provide a bit more information in Chapter 12 about these plans along with resources for you to learn more.

• The information in the book is believed to be current as of the date of publication but as with all subject matters, information may change or be interpreted differently over time.

• You should refer to the 529 plan's most current offering materials (sometimes referred to as a program disclosure statement, plan or program description, or as an offering statement, booklet or circular), which are typically available on or through the plan's home page for official information about a particular 529 plan. You may also obtain a copy by contacting a plan representative if you are investing directly with the plan or by contacting a financial professional if you are working with one.

• The information in this book is believed to be accurate but it is possible that the text contains inadvertent mistakes or typographical errors.

- This guide is intended to provide you with general information and is in no way intended to serve as investment, tax, legal, or other professional advice. A trusted advisor or financial professional who is familiar with your particular situation, goals, and objectives should be consulted as needed for advice and guidance on investment, tax, coordination with other benefits, and/or legal matters.

CHAPTER 1

START WITH YOUR DESTINATION IN MIND: EMBRACING YOUR *WHY* AS YOU BEGIN YOUR SAVINGS JOURNEY

When you begin a trip by car or purchase a ticket for a plane or train, you have the end point in mind and you've undoubtedly taken time to select your destination, envisioning how your trip will turn out. Likewise, as you begin the process of saving for college, starting with the end in mind is a powerful place to begin. While it may feel entirely too early to imagine what your child will want to pursue after high school, you can certainly imagine the quality of life and experiences that you will want education to afford your child. You can also imagine the position you will want to be in to help your child pursue their dreams, whatever they may be.

Research suggests that visualizing desired outcomes and imagining how they will feel when achieved can be an extremely helpful initial step when establishing goals and can also be valuable for maintaining momentum along the way. In the case of saving for a child's higher education, reminding yourself why you value education is a great starting point. The options, opportunities, and independence that higher education will afford your child may be part of your vision. Your vision may also include a rewarding career for your child as well as financial security. Your vision for your child will be based on your values, your dreams, and your definition of success.

1

Your vision will be unique to you and your family. And the clearer it is, the more achievable it will become.

Additionally, taking time to think about what you want your family's experience to be (and just as importantly, what you don't want it to be) when it comes time to pay for college or career training is an important first step. Perhaps you want to be in a position to experience the peace of mind that comes with having done your best to prepare. Perhaps you want to have saved enough money for your child(ren) to have the flexibility to pursue the types of schools or majors that align well with their interests and passions, which will lead to work they really love. Or, perhaps you would like to be in a position to have helped your child(ren) begin adult life debt-free with an open freeway of options ahead of them as they begin their lives as independent adults.

Once you become clear about what you want the experience to look like, cultivating how it will feel to achieve it can help tremendously as well. Here are some questions you might ask yourself to begin to define your vision of how you'd like the future to look and feel:

- What do I value about education and why?

- What do I hope education will provide my child(ren)? For instance, is it your wish that education will provide your child a deeper understanding of the world, a sense of purpose, skills to pursue a rewarding career, increased earnings potential, a healthy lifestyle, an opportunity to develop new skills, the flexibility to pursue their calling, or to enjoy a more rewarding career than your own?

● To what extent do I want my child(ren) and/or others to contribute to the funding process?

● How will I feel knowing my child or I won't (or will) need to take on considerable educational debt to pursue academic and career goals?

● How will I handle the regret of not establishing a plan?

● To what extent will student loans impact the vision I have for my child's future?

You'll be more likely to get started and to stick to your savings plan if you embrace a specific mental picture of how you and your family will feel about being prepared for your child's post-secondary education expenses and the value education will provide to your child. Keeping these images top of mind will keep you motivated and committed to your goal.

Whatever your *Why* is comprised of, making a written note of it is a great place to begin, and also a wonderful place to revisit to keep you committed to the saving process. Be sure to note what you value about education and how you'd like your future to look and feel.

MY **VISION**

"When we know what our goals in life are, we set our priorities accordingly. And as long as we keep them in sight, we won't be as likely to turn back or lose the trail."
—Joshua Becker, *The Minimalist Home*[3]

In Chapter 6, *Planning Your Trip and Developing Your Roadmap: Considering Your Time Horizon, Risk Tolerance, and Investment Objectives*, you'll learn how to forecast the cost of the type of education you want to provide your child and how much it will take to get you there. And in Chapter 7, *Staying on Course: Incorporating Tips and Tricks to Keep on Track and to Remind You that You're in the Driver's Seat*, you'll learn the value of breaking your goal into bite size steps as well as other strategies to help keep you on track.

A Peek into My Journey

As a married couple with multiple degrees between us, my husband and I were deep in educational debt when our son arrived five and a half years into our marriage. Knowing first-hand the stress associated with accumulating and repaying undergraduate and graduate school debt provided strong motivation for us to work together to achieve a more favorable outcome for our son.

We were committed to doing all we could to avoid reliving, directly or indirectly, the stressful experience and consequences of being financially unprepared for higher education.

---

[3] Becker, Joshua. *The Minimalist Home: A Room-by-Room Guide to a Decluttered, Refocused Life.* WaterBrook, 1st Edition, December 2018.

Beyond this, we wanted our son to have options about which school to attend, what majors to consider, and ultimately, what career to pursue. We wanted him to enter adulthood without being weighed down by student loan debt as we once were. Lastly, we really wanted to be able to sleep well at night knowing we were doing everything we could to be prepared.

KEY TAKE-AWAYS

❏ Getting clear on your *Why—seeing* and *feeling* how you want your and your child's experience to be—will help you stick to your goals.

❏ After visualizing what you want and cultivating how it will feel, taking actions to support your goals will get you where you want to be.

❏ If you can see it, you can believe it and achieve it.

CHAPTER 2

GETTING OFF THE SIDELINES AND ON THE ROAD: RECOGNIZING THAT NOW IS THE TIME TO PLAN FOR TOMORROW

Once you've established and embraced your *Why*, it's time to address the *How* and to get started as soon as possible. You simply cannot afford to keep hitting the snooze button on saving for college. While time is on your side, determining how you will get from where you are to where you want to be will require a plan, a roadmap so to speak. The sooner you get started saving for your child's education, the better. The time is now no matter how old your children are.

Parents of Older Children. For those with older children, please don't be discouraged. The point is that you've found this book and you are starting now—that's 100 percent better than not starting at all. You can look for ways to trim your current budget to save as much as possible and you can invite others to contribute as well. See Chapter 9, *Creating a Travel Budget: Saving More by Spending Less and Incorporating Minimalism* and Chapter 10, *Realizing You Don't Need to Travel Alone: Engaging Others to Join You on Your Journey.* Every dollar you save and invest now is that much less that you will have to borrow and repay with interest later.

Parents of Younger Children. For those of you with younger children, don't fall into the trap of delaying the savings process because the future seems so distant. Instead of thinking of college as being 18 long years away, consider that there are only 6,570 days between your child's birth and 18th birthday. And, in fact, more than 2,100 of those days will be behind you by the time your child is six. It's never too early to start planning for the future.

Saving with 529 College Savings Plans. In terms of *how* to save, the focus of this book is largely on 529 college savings plans, one of the most popular and effective tools there is. You'll have a chance to look under the hood and gain a comprehensive understanding of these plans in Chapter 3, *Know Before You Go: Examining Tax Benefits and Other Features that Make 529 a Preferred Route* and Chapter 4, *Understanding the Terrain: Debunking the Most Common Myths Regarding 529 College Savings Plans*, and throughout many other sections of this book.

There are certainly other ways to save for college—including 529 prepaid tuition plans which have many of the same tax benefits as 529 college savings plans. You'll learn about these and other savings vehicles in Chapter 12, *Considering Alternate Routes: A Look at Other Ways to Save.* I am focusing on 529 college savings plans because they are the college planning vehicle that I am most familiar with and they are exactly what I have used to successfully save in-full for my son's higher education.

What could possibly get in the way of your getting started? There are countless reasons you may come up with to stay on the sidelines and not get on the road. I'll address some of the most common excuses and give you my thoughts on each.

Don't have the time. The small investment of time you spend getting started NOW by opening and beginning to fund an account is time well spent, and it will help you avoid years of regret about not having gotten started sooner. Many plans enable you to sign up online often in 10–15 minutes. One small step today can make a significant difference in the quality of your life and your child's for years to come. Far too many potential savers waste valuable time waffling for years about whether or how to start saving for college, and ultimately take no action.

Don't have the money. Many plans allow you to get started with as little as $25—or even less—and opening an account enables you to invite others to contribute even if you can't contribute very much right now. Plus, saving and investing even small amounts of money over time, thanks to the power of compound earnings, can make a big difference when it comes time to pay for education after high school. Coupled with the tax benefits of 529 college savings plans, the impact can be even greater.

Confused about how the plans work. This book should answer most of your questions. In a nutshell, 529 college savings plans allow you to invest money into a special account for the benefit of a future student, and the account grows tax-free. When you withdraw funds, you will not need to pay tax on any of the earnings when they're used to pay for a wide range of approved educational expenses.

Don't know where to begin. There is an abundance of information online and the steps to get started are easy to follow. One of the easiest first steps is to take a look at your state's 529 plan. With the exception of Wyoming, every state, along with the District of Columbia, has a 529 college savings plan. And, if you happen to have a trusted financial professional in your life, you can begin by asking that person for advice on which option would be appropriate for you. More on this in Chapter 5, *Going it Alone or Asking for Directions: Considering Direct-to-Consumer Versus Advisor-Sold College Savings Plans.*

Not sure my child will pursue education after high school. While it may be far too early to assess what your child's career aspirations may be, almost all possibilities will require some form of training and education. Not planning for future educational expenses could harm your family financially and could cause you and/or your child to take out significant student loans, a decision you and your child may later regret as you struggle to repay them. See Chapter 16, *Rough Road Ahead: Examining the Cost of Missing the On-Ramp and Not Planning Ahead.*

Feels overwhelming. Don't panic. Plan. Making a plan to save and pay for college doesn't have to be difficult nor does it have to be a solo act. With time on your side, you can break your goal into manageable small steps. You can also engage your friends, family, and even your employer to lend a hand once you have your account established. And in age-appropriate ways, your child can pitch in as well.

I can understand that for any of the reasons listed above, you may be reluctant to get started and that it may feel hard to do so. I'd be remiss, however, if I didn't tell you that pushing through your resistance now will be considerably easier than carrying an incredible weight of regret with you for years to come. **The future will come whether you are prepared for it or not. Don't miss the opportunity to be in the driver's seat and to help design an outcome that you and your family will celebrate versus regret.**

"You are one decision away from a completely different life."

—Mel Robbins, *The 5 Second Rule*[4]

A Peek into My Journey

It wasn't at all clear that it would be feasible for my husband and I to even afford having a child, let alone begin funding a 529 college savings account while we were still paying back over $100,000 in undergraduate and graduate school loans of our own.

Nonetheless, we managed to do so. If we had thought too long or hard about our collective educational debt, about the new expense of full-time childcare or about rapidly outgrowing our small apartment, we would have never begun saving. While we couldn't see clearly

---

[4] Robbins, Mel. *The 5 Second Rule: Transform Your Life, Work, and Confidence with Everyday Courage.* Savio Republic, February 2017.

what the future would hold during those long days and sometimes sleepless nights of first-time parenthood, we followed our instincts about what would likely be needed down the road and how we would want to feel in the future. And boy, are we glad we did.

We resisted laboring too long over the various 529 college savings program choices and the vast array of investment options within each plan, though we very easily could have (as we did with other decisions such as which car seat was safest, which baby monitor to choose, and so on). Instead, we made a selection that seemed right for us and started by depositing small cash gifts we received for our son's birth and baptism.

Because we were exhausted and somewhat overwhelmed as new parents, the decision to get started by opening a 529 account felt like the hardest step, although it took very little time once we sat down to do it. In retrospect, taking those few minutes to open our 529 account was one of the very best decisions we made early in our son's life, and that decision continues to pay off in countless ways. It was a small amount of time that was very well spent.

KEY TAKE-AWAYS

❑ There are many excuses to postpone getting started, but there are even more reasons to start saving.

❑ When saving for a long-term goal like higher education, you'll have a better chance of meeting your objectives when you have time on your side. It's never too early or too late to start.

❑ It's easy to begin. In many cases, 10–15 minutes and $25 (or even less) can get you started. The information you need is easy to find online.

❑ If you happen to have a financial professional with whom you already work, mention that you'd like to open a 529 college savings account.

❑ Your future self (and child) will thank you for starting NOW.

5 SIMPLE STEPS
TO **GET STARTED**

☐ Determine your **WHY.**

☐ Explore the basics of 529 college savings plans.

☐ Open an account online on your own (you'll typically need no more than 15 minutes and $25 or even less) or with the help of an advisor, if you have one.

☐ Set up automatic contributions.

☐ Tell friends, family (and your employer) about your mission to save and invite them to contribute.

CHAPTER 3

KNOW BEFORE YOU GO: EXAMINING TAX BENEFITS AND OTHER FEATURES THAT MAKE 529 A PREFERRED ROUTE

By way of background, 529 college savings plans got their name from the provision (Section 529) of the Internal Revenue Code that authorized them. These plans are established and maintained by states or state agencies, some of which manage most aspects of the plans on their own while others engage and oversee experienced financial services and investment firms (often referred to as program or investment managers) to manage the investments in the plans, to provide customer support, to help with marketing and sales, and to perform other important functions.

There are many features of 529 college savings plans that make them a popular way to save for education after high school. Some of the features that investors appreciate most include the ability to:

- Save on taxes while saving for education—earnings aren't subject to federal or state tax when used for covered expenses

- Get started with a low initial deposit, typically $25 or even less

- Save for anyone—it doesn't have to be a son, daughter, or even a relative

- Open an account without state residency or income requirements

- Conveniently earmark funds for higher education and avoid the temptation to use the money for other priorities

- Use accounts at a wide range of post-secondary schools across the United States including two-year and four-year colleges, graduate schools, trade schools, and some international options as well

- Cover a broad range of educational expenses such as tuition, fees, books, supplies, computers, and certain apprenticeship and room and board costs

Here are additional details:

Federal Tax Savings. 529 college savings accounts grow tax-free and are never taxed when used for qualified purposes. Less tax means more money for college. After-tax dollars are contributed to 529 college savings accounts and while not federally tax deductible, there may be state tax deductions or credits available to you. See State Tax Savings section below and additional details in the Appendix.

There are two components to the federal tax savings available to you with 529 college savings plans:

The first component results from the deferral of income as your account grows in value. Any interest or investment gain on account contributions is tax-deferred (not taxed while in the account).

The second component results when monies are withdrawn from the account. When you make a withdrawal from the account, there is no tax due on earnings as long as the amount withdrawn is used for the beneficiary's covered educational expenses (more formally referred to as "Qualified Higher Education Expenses"—see definition below).

This favorable tax treatment for 529 college savings plans differs from standard investments, which are typically taxed on interest, dividends, and capital gains as account values grow **and** are taxed when withdrawals are made if sold at a profit. As long as 529 college savings accounts are used for covered expenses, no tax is owed on the gain upon distribution of funds. It's important to note, however, that while the earnings on 529 college savings accounts always grow tax-deferred, if distributions from your account are not used for covered expenses, the earnings portion (but not the full value) of the withdrawal may be subject to federal and state tax, as well as a 10% federal penalty on the earnings. You can read more about the tax treatment of non-qualified withdrawals and special exceptions in Chapter 13, *Keeping Your Eyes on the Road: Risks & Special Considerations.*

State Tax Savings. In addition to the wonderful federal tax benefits that are consistent across all plans, nearly two-thirds of the states offer favorable state tax benefits for 529 plan investors. In fact, 27 states as well as the District of Columbia offer residents a personal income tax deduction or credit for contributions made to that state's 529 college savings plan. Seven states go even a step further and offer a deduction or credit for contributions to the state's 529 college savings plan or to *any* other state's plan. State tax deductions or credits range from $150 to unlimited and are subject to certain conditions. As an added bonus in some states, if the amount contributed to a 529 college savings plan in a particular year exceeds the amount permitted for a particular state tax credit or deduction, the remainder can be carried over and applied as a credit or deduction in subsequent years.

In the Appendix you will find a listing of states that currently have state tax deductions or credits in place for 529 college savings plan contributions and the current amount of these deductions or credits. While the chart provides initial information about the existence and value of current deductions or credits, it is important for you to check with your state's 529 plan to confirm the specific conditions for deductions or credits. For instance, you'll want to confirm who may take the deduction or credit. In some states, only the account owner or the account owner's spouse may take the deduction and in other states, any contributor who is a state taxpayer may take the deduction or credit.

• The 27 states that offer state tax deductions or credits for contributions to their own state program are: Alabama, Colorado, Connecticut, Georgia, Idaho, Illinois, Indiana, Iowa, Louisiana, Maryland, Massachusetts, Michigan, Mississippi, Nebraska, New Mexico, New York, North Dakota, Ohio, Oklahoma, Oregon, Rhode Island, South Carolina, Utah, Vermont, Virginia, West

Virginia, and Wisconsin. The District of Columbia falls into this category as well.

• The seven states that go a bit further and offer state tax deductions or credits for contributions to their own state program (or any other state's 529 college savings program) are: Arizona, Arkansas, Kansas, Minnesota, Missouri, Montana, and Pennsylvania.

• The states that do not offer a state tax deduction or credit for contributions to 529 college savings plan are: Alaska, California, Delaware, Florida, Hawaii, Kentucky, Maine, Nevada, New Hampshire, New Jersey, North Carolina, South Dakota, Tennessee, Texas, Washington, and Wyoming.

Don't see your state mentioned as having a state tax benefit? If your state does not have a state tax deduction or credit for contributions to a 529 college savings plan, there may be other state-specific benefits for you to consider. Take a look at what else it has to offer and compare it to other states' 529 college savings plans. Regardless of the state tax treatment of the plan you ultimately select, you'll enjoy the same federal tax treatment as discussed earlier. And, you can invest in more than one plan. More on this in Chapter 15, *Taking the Scenic Route: Exploring Advanced Applications of 529 College Savings Plans.*

Other State Benefits. In addition to or instead of state tax deductions and/or credits, some states offer valuable state-specific benefits such as scholarships, grants, or matching funds, favorable state financial aid treatment, employer incentives, and protection from creditors to those residents who invest in the state's own 529 college savings plan. Others offer special programs to help families get started. Be sure to identify and consider these as you are deciding in which plan to invest, remembering you are not limited to just one plan.

Keep in mind that state-based benefits are one of many appropriately weighted factors to consider when making an investment decision.

Wide Range of Covered Educational Expenses. These are referred to as *Qualified Higher Education Expenses* and they include:

- **Tuition**

- **Mandatory fees**

- **Books**

- **Supplies**

- **Equipment**

Note: the above expenses must be required for enrollment or attendance by eligible post-secondary schools (referred to as *Eligible Educational Institutions* and defined below).

- **Room and board**

Room and board is a covered expense for students who are enrolled at least half-time at eligible schools. In addition to the cost of living on campus and utilizing campus food services, costs associated with living off campus and at home are covered expenses as well, up to their actual cost or the college's published cost of attendance allowance for room and board, whichever is less.

- **Registered Apprenticeship Program covered expenses**

These are expenses that are required for participation in registered apprenticeship programs. To qualify, these programs must be registered and certified with the Secretary of Labor under Section 1 of the National Apprenticeship Act.

- **Computers, Software, Peripheral Equipment, and Internet Access**

Covered expenses also include the purchase of computer or peripheral equipment, computer software or internet access, and related services if it's to be used primarily by the beneficiary during any of the years that the beneficiary is enrolled at an Eligible Educational Institution. Understandably, unless predominantly educational in nature, computer software for sports, games, or hobbies is not a covered expense.

- **Special Needs Services**

Additional covered expenses include services required by an individual with special needs in connection with enrollment or attendance at an Eligible Educational Institution.

Wide Range of Educational Options. Eligible Educational Institutions include a broad range of options such as accredited two-year and four-year public and private post-secondary educational institutions, as well as proprietary and vocational schools that offer credit toward an associate degree, a bachelor's degree, a professional or graduate level degree, or some other form of post-secondary credential and that are eligible to receive federal financial aid.

Nearly all accredited institutions are eligible. To see which U.S. and international schools have Federal School Codes—an identification number used with federal financial aid program-eligible schools— check the U.S. Department of Education's website, fafsa.ed.gov. You may also contact a particular school to determine if it qualifies as an eligible educational institution.

Easy to Get Started. Once you've decided to move forward, opening a 529 college savings account can take as little as 10–15 minutes.

Here's the information you will need to open an account:

1. **Account owner name and contact information** (permanent mailing address and email address)

Note: The *account owner* is the adult who will control the account. This could be you, your spouse or partner, a grandparent, or someone else. The account owner does not need to be the parent of the future student (the beneficiary) for whom the account is being established. In fact, the account owner does not need to be related to the beneficiary.

2. Beneficiary name

Note: The *beneficiary* (more formally referred to as a *designated beneficiary*) is the future student who will use the funds to pay for higher education expenses.

3. Date of birth and social security (or individual taxpayer identification) number for both the account owner and beneficiary

4. Banking Information (optional)

Note: If you want to set up automatic contributions through bank transfer, you will need to have your checking or savings account number and your bank's routing number.

5. Successor Account Owner name and contact information (optional, but highly recommended)

Note: You may want to appoint a successor account owner to take over control of the account in the event of your death or mental incapacity.

You may always add or change bank instructions for automatic contributions and a successor account owner at a later date.

Many Plans to Choose From. There are many 529 college savings plans to choose from with a wide range of investment options, contribution limits and other features and benefits. Nearly every state has at least one 529 college savings option, and some have several. Nine states currently have prepaid tuition programs as well. You're very likely to find a 529 option that's right for you. In addition to visiting specific state 529 plan websites to learn more, there are a number of online tools that can help you compare 529 college savings plans. More on this in Chapter 6, *Planning Your Trip and Developing Your Roadmap: Considering Your Time Horizon, Risk Tolerance, and Investment Objectives.*

No Age Restrictions. There are no age restrictions on the beneficiary.

No Time Constraints. There are no required distributions and generally no restrictions on the length of time the account can remain open.

No Income Restrictions. There are no income restrictions on the account owner or beneficiary. 529 college savings accounts are useful for families of all income levels.

Low Initial Minimums. In many cases, you can get started with as little as $25 and in some cases, even less.

Low Subsequent Contribution Minimums. Many plans allow you to make contributions of $25 or less after you open the account.

High Maximum Contribution and Balance Limits. Many 529 plans have maximum lifetime contribution or balance limits that exceed $250,000 per beneficiary and some go as high as $500,000+. That means contributions can be made until the total contributions for a particular beneficiary reaches the lifetime maximum contribution limit or until the balance on the account reaches a lifetime balance limit.

Others Can Contribute Too. Friends, family, and even employers can contribute up to $15,000 annually to your account. Learn more about this in Chapter 10, *Realizing You Don't Need to Travel Alone: Engaging Others to Join You on Your Journey.* Additional information on employer involvement can be found in Chapter 15, *Taking the Scenic Route: Exploring Advanced Applications of 529 College Savings Plans.*

Control. Even though the account is established for the benefit of a future student—the beneficiary—and contributions are generally considered completed gifts to the beneficiary, the account owner retains complete control of the account at all times. This enables the account owner to assure the funds are used for the intended purpose. The account owner decides whether and when to withdraw funds for the beneficiary's use and can change the beneficiary on the account at any time. This is different than custodial accounts (UGMA/UTMA) in which account control switches to the beneficiary at the age of termination—typically age 18 or 21 depending on state law.

Further, while the value of account contributions are removed from the taxable estate of the account owner and viewed as completed gifts to the beneficiary for estate tax purposes, because of the unique control that a 529 college savings plan account owner has over the account, the owner has the ability to revoke the gift, and return the assets to the account owner's taxable estate. I know of no other investment vehicle that provides this unique combination of control and estate reduction.

Annual Gift Tax Exclusion and Completed Gifts. There's no federal gift tax on contributions up to $15,000 per beneficiary per year. These contributions qualify for the annual gift tax exclusion (currently $15,000 for individuals, and $30,000 for spouses who split gifts; this is periodically adjusted for inflation). As mentioned in the previous section on control, contributions to 529 college savings plans are considered completed gifts to the beneficiary and are removed from the donor's estate. More on this in Chapter 15, *Taking the Scenic Route: Exploring Advanced Applications of 529 College Savings Plans.*

Five-Year Gift Averaging (sometimes referred to as Five-Year Forward Gifting or Accelerated Gifting). Rather than simply contributing up to $15,000 a year, you or others may make a one-time gift equivalent to a maximum of up to five years of contributions to a 529 college savings account and still qualify for the federal gift tax exclusion by electing to prorate the contribution against the annual gift tax exclusion over a period of five years ratably. More on this in Chapter 15, *Taking the Scenic Route: Exploring Advanced Applications of 529 College Savings Plans.*

Other Expenses that Can Be Covered. While not the focus of this book, it's important to note that 529 college savings plans can be used for both K–12 tuition and for student loan repayment, subject to limitations.

- **K–12 Tuition.** Up to $10,000 per year per beneficiary can be withdrawn from 529 college savings accounts to cover tuition required for enrollment or attendance at an elementary or secondary public, private, or religious school. For such withdrawals, there will be no federal tax or penalty owed on the account earnings, however, state tax treatment varies and you should confirm with your state what, if any, state tax or penalties may be imposed.

- **Student Loan Repayment.** Up to $10,000 over the life of the 529 college savings account can be withdrawn to pay toward principal or interest for qualified student loans of a 529 account's beneficiary or the beneficiary's brother, sister, stepbrother, or stepsister. For such withdrawals, there will be no federal tax or penalty owed on the account earnings, however, state tax treatment varies and you should confirm with your state what, if any, state tax or penalties may be imposed.

Useful for Entities Too. 529 college savings plan accounts can be opened not only by individuals, but by entities as well. They are easier to administer than trust accounts for non-profits and other entities with scholarship or children's savings account (CSA) programs. You'll learn in Chapter 15, *Taking the Scenic Route: Exploring Advanced Applications of 529 College Savings Plans* how non-profits and other entities can use these accounts to invest scholarship funds for future students.

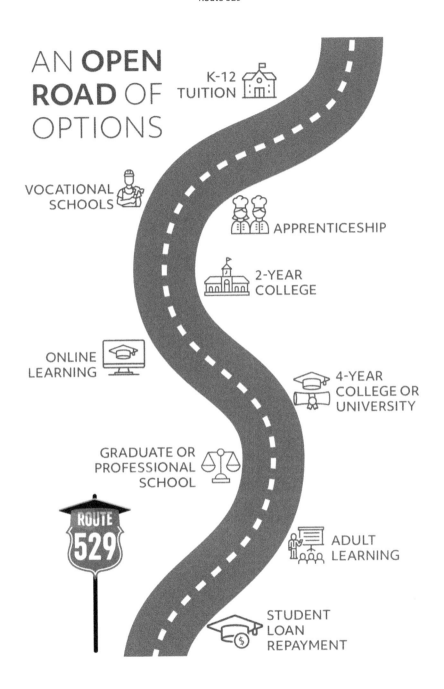

AN **OPEN ROAD** OF OPTIONS

K-12 TUITION

VOCATIONAL SCHOOLS

APPRENTICESHIP

2-YEAR COLLEGE

ONLINE LEARNING

4-YEAR COLLEGE OR UNIVERSITY

GRADUATE OR PROFESSIONAL SCHOOL

ROUTE 529

ADULT LEARNING

STUDENT LOAN REPAYMENT

KEY TAKE-AWAYS

❑ 529 college savings plans are not just for college. They can be used for a wide range of educational expenses at a wide range of post-secondary institutions for a wide range of degree programs.

❑ Low minimums make it easy to get started. High maximums help you save significant amounts.

❑ The earnings on contributions to these accounts grow tax-free and are never taxed if used for covered expenses. Covered expenses include tuition, fees, room and board, books, supplies, and more. Paying less tax can result in more money for college.

❑ You are not limited to investing in your home state plan or the state plan where your beneficiary resides. It is, however, advisable to check your home state 529 college savings program(s) to see if there are particular state tax or other benefits that you might miss by investing in an out-of-state plan. State-based benefits are one of many appropriately weighted factors to consider.

❑ You may invest in more than one 529 college savings plan, including prepaid tuition plans.

❑ 529 college savings plans allow the account owner to retain complete control even though contributions to these accounts are considered completed gifts.

CHAPTER 4

UNDERSTANDING THE TERRAIN: DEBUNKING THE MOST COMMON MYTHS REGARDING 529 COLLEGE SAVINGS PLANS

Here are the most common myths you may hear when considering an investment in a 529 college savings plan. It's important to know the facts.

Myth 1: 529 college savings plans can only be used for traditional four-year colleges. This is FALSE.

Fact: Withdrawals from 529 college savings plans can be used for a wide range of institutions including two-year, four-year, trade and technical, graduate, and professional schools, and in connection with registered and certified apprenticeships.

Myth 2: A 529 college savings plan beneficiary must attend school in the state offering the 529 plan. This is FALSE.

Fact: Funds can be used at eligible institutions around the country regardless of which state's 529 college savings plan the account is held.

Myth 3: You need a lot of money to get started. This is FALSE.

Fact: Many 529 college savings plans allow you to get started with as little as $25, and even less in some cases.

Myth 4: You will forfeit the value of your investment if your child does not attend college. This is FALSE.

Fact: Your account value is never forfeited. It always belongs to you, the account owner. If the beneficiary for whom the account was established decides to not pursue higher education immediately after high school (or at all), you have several options:

a. At any time, you can change the beneficiary to another student or future student (as long as the student is a *family member* of the original beneficiary). This is a broad range of related persons and includes a beneficiary's future children. It may even include the account owner, depending on the relationship with the beneficiary.

Members of the beneficiary's family include the beneficiary's spouse and the following other relatives of the beneficiary:

1. Son, daughter, stepchild, foster child, adopted child, or a descendant of any of them
2. Brother, sister, stepbrother, or stepsister
3. Father or mother, or ancestor of either
4. Stepfather or stepmother
5. Son or daughter of a brother or sister
6. Brother or sister of father or mother
7. Son-in-law, daughter-in-law, father-in-law, mother-in-law, brother-in-law, or sister-in-law
8. The spouse of any individual listed above
9. First cousin

b. Leave the money invested as most plans do not have maximum timeframes in which assets must be used. Account beneficiaries sometimes change their minds about whether and when to pursue higher education. You may keep the money invested while your child sorts out which path to take. It may be comforting to remember that the above list of family members includes your child's future children. So, if your child doesn't use the money, you can save it for a future grandchild if you wish.

c. Withdraw the money for non-educational purposes of any kind and pay state, federal, and local ordinary income tax only on the earnings portion (which you had not paid while the assets were growing in the account tax-deferred) and a 10% federal penalty only on the earnings portion of the withdrawal. You will not pay tax on the contribution portion of your withdrawal.

Myth 5: You will be penalized or will forfeit your savings if your child receives a full or partial scholarship. This is FALSE.

Fact: If the beneficiary for whom the 529 college savings account was established receives a full or partial scholarship or attends a military academy, you can withdraw up to the amount of the scholarship from your account if you feel you will not need that money for other covered expenses. The withdrawal will be subject to applicable tax on the earnings portion at the recipient's tax rate (since taxes were deferred while invested). However, withdrawals made based on receipt of scholarships are not subject to the additional federal penalty. Alternatively, you may keep in the money in the account for future use. See the Fact section of Myth 4 for additional options.

Myth 6: The value of 529 college savings plan accounts will have a significant adverse impact on federal financial aid eligibility. This is FALSE.

Fact: Saving in 529 college savings plans has very little impact, if any, on need-based federal financial aid eligibility. A student's financial need is the difference between a post-secondary school's cost of attendance and the amount that a student's family is expected to contribute (referred to as Expected Family Contribution or EFC). The most significant factor in calculating Expected Family Contribution is parents' annual income—not parental assets—such as 529 college savings accounts.

When 529 accounts are owned by a parent (which they often are), they are treated as parental assets for financial aid calculation purposes. They are reported on the Free Application for Federal Student Aid (FAFSA) as a parental asset. As such, the value of the 529 college savings account may only reduce a student's need-based financial aid package by a maximum of 5.64% of the 529 account value.

For example, if you save $10,000, only $564 will be included in a family's Expected Family Contribution (EFC) for federal financial aid purposes. This is far lower than the potential 20% rate that is assessed on student assets such as those held in UGMA/UTMA custodial accounts.

While schools and institutions may undertake their own financial aid analysis in addition to the FAFSA and may count 529 plans in need-based analysis, it's still better to save than not to save. In fact, some forms of aid, such as loans, require repayment. Many parents do not realize that when schools issue financial aid packages, they include student loans that need to be repaid with interest, not simply grants, scholarships, or work study that require no repayment. You'll be avoiding or reducing your reliance on student loan debt by preparing in advance for college costs.

Myth 7: There's no need to save because college will be free and/or full scholarships will be easy to obtain. This is FALSE.

Fact: The likelihood of a full scholarship that covers all costs of higher education is very slim. Additionally, while some states, cities, and regions do indeed have free or reduced tuition programs, keep in mind that many of these programs typically only cover the cost of tuition and do not cover the cost of room and board, books, supplies, equipment, computers, or other expenses required by the university or college. These additional expenses can really add up. Also, these free tuition programs often have strict eligibility provisions that are frequently linked to income and to particular schools at which courses can be taken.

Even if you feel your child may receive a scholarship or be eligible for free tuition someday, it is still valuable to plan ahead for the additional costs that will be involved in pursuing a degree. These costs can include everything from books to supplies, equipment to academic fees, to room and board. Even with the most generous of awards, parents are typically required to contribute toward the cost of their child's education. Also, as you will learn in Chapter 14, *Sites You Won't Want to Miss: Considering the Often-Overlooked Additional Benefits of Saving for College*, saving for college is beneficial in other ways as well.

Myth 8: The beneficiary of the 529 account must be my own child. This is FALSE.

Fact: The beneficiary on a 529 college savings account does not need to be your child or related to you at all. While your beneficiary could be your child, it could also be your grandchild, niece or nephew, someone unrelated, or even you.

Myth 9: I am locked into the investment option I first select. This is FALSE.

Fact: You can change your investment direction for your existing contributions twice annually and you can always change investment choices upon a change in your beneficiary to a member of that beneficiary's family (as described in the Fact section of Myth 4). For new contributions to your account, you can always make new investment choices. You can also change your plan entirely by rolling over to another plan. A rollover for the benefit of the same beneficiary or for the benefit of a member of the beneficiary's family is allowed once in every 12-month period subject to conditions.

Myth 10: I need to wait for my child to be born before I can open an account. This is FALSE.

Fact: You can open an account and name yourself as both the account owner and the designated beneficiary and then, switch the beneficiary to your child once you have a date of birth and social security number. It is, however, very important to remember to change the beneficiary from you to your child as soon as possible following arrival. Depending on the investment style you selected, the age of the beneficiary may be an important factor with respect to how the assets in the account are invested.

Myth 11: There are income restrictions on who can invest. This is FALSE.

Fact: Families with incomes of any amount can plan ahead for the cost of higher education with 529 college savings plans.

Myth 12: I cannot use a tax identification number to open an account. This is FALSE.

Fact: While you need to be a U.S. citizen or resident alien to open an account, you can open an account with *either* a tax identification number or social security number.

Myth 13: 529 plans have very high fees. This is FALSE.

Fact: Fees on 529 college savings plans have declined over the years and in many cases, are quite reasonable given the access to professional investment management services typically received with these plans. Fees and expenses vary across plans and investment types and should always be a consideration. See Chapter 13, *Keeping Your Eyes on the Road: Risks & Special Considerations.*

Myth 14: If I invest in a 529 college savings plan, I cannot save in other types of accounts for higher education expenses. This is FALSE.

Fact: 529 college savings plans can be a complement to other savings vehicles such as 529 prepaid tuition plans, as well as other investment vehicles like Coverdell Education Savings accounts. You can learn more about other options in Chapter 12, *Considering Alternate Routes: A Look at Other Ways to Save.*

Myth 15: You or your beneficiary must be a resident of the same state as the 529 college savings plan you select. This is FALSE.

Fact: In almost all cases, there are no residency requirements to invest in a particular 529 college savings plan. You may invest in your home state's 529 and/or in another state's plan. It's always good to examine your own state's plan in addition to others you may consider.

Myth 16: It's too late to start saving once my child is in high school. This is FALSE.

Fact: It's never too late to open an account and start investing. 529 college savings plans have no age limits and have options that are appropriate no matter where you are on your time horizon. Even if you invest for just a few years, with tax-deferred growth and tax-free withdrawals for qualified purposes, you'll have more resources for education than you otherwise would have had. Family and friends can contribute too. Whatever you manage to save will be that much less that you or your child will need to borrow and repay with interest. And remember, you can continue to save while your child is in college.

KEY TAKE-AWAYS

❑ Don't let misinformation deter or confuse you.

❑ To confirm details, check 529 college savings plan websites or offering materials for the most accurate and up-to-date information.

❑ Understanding the facts about 529 college savings plans will empower you.

CHAPTER 5

GOING IT ALONE OR ASKING FOR DIRECTIONS: CONSIDERING DIRECT-TO-CONSUMER VERSUS ADVISOR-SOLD COLLEGE SAVINGS PLANS

There are two primary ways to invest in 529 college savings plans. Either route can get you where you need to be if you get started and commit to contributing regularly.

One way is with the help of a financial professional and the other way is to invest on your own by using comprehensive information that is provided online or which you can request and acquire by mail. Either way works fine depending on your personal preferences and financial comfort level. Millions of families have invested on their own (directly with 529 college savings plans) using tools and resources made available by the plans, and millions of others have invested with the help of financial professionals. There's no one way to go.

Investing on Your Own. Those who simply want to invest in professionally designed pre-packaged or ready-made investment options based on a child's age or anticipated enrollment date (described in Chapter 6) or who are comfortable conducting their own research and making and monitoring their own investment selections may wish to consider enrolling on their own in a direct-to-consumer 529 plan. The enrollment can be done in under 15 minutes by completing an application on a 529 plan website. To sign up, you'll need the social security number (or tax identification number), address, and date of birth for both the account owner and the future student (the beneficiary). If you are saving for more than one future student, you will need to open a separate account for each.

A wide range of 529 college savings plans are available and within each plan, a wide range of investment options are available as well. A good place to consider starting is with your home state's plan (currently 49 states and the District of Columbia have 529 college savings plans to choose from). If you are not familiar with options that your home state may have, you can do a quick internet search using the name of your state and the words "529 college savings plan". You'll find that some states have more than one plan from which to choose. Nearly every state has an option that you can enroll in directly and some also have an option that you can enroll in if you decide to do so with the help of a financial professional (see section below—Working with a Financial Services Professional).

You may also want to visit www.collegesavings.org (The College Savings Plans Network) or savingforcollege.com to see a list of plan options across all states and to explore ones that may be right for you. You can compare plans based on state tax and other state-specific benefits, investment managers, available investment options, fees and expenses, and other factors. If you are working with a financial professional, that person can help you compare and contrast plans with a wide range of factors in mind.

After you select a 529 college savings plan, you'll need to pick an investment option. More on this in Chapter 6, *Planning Your Trip and Developing Your Roadmap: Considering Your Time Horizon, Risk Tolerance, and Investment Objectives.* While customer service representatives at 529 college savings plan call centers cannot provide you with personalized investment advice, they can answer questions you may have about the plan(s) they offer.

Those who need guidance in navigating college savings choices, prefer to have their educational goals considered together with their other financial goals, desire support for monitoring their investments and staying the course in times of market volatility and/or who need or desire a more custom-designed investing approach may benefit from working with a financial services professional.

Working with a Financial Services Professional. Financial advisors, investment advisor, financial planners, and other financial professionals—sometimes referred to as investment or financial consultants—can be extremely helpful to those planning ahead for higher education expenses. They not only help clients select a suitable investment vehicle and strategy for higher education financing, they can also provide advice regarding a family's overall financial picture.

In addition to monitoring your investments, financial advisors can recommend adjustments that may be needed in light of any changes in your circumstances, market conditions, and/or projected costs so you can stay on track with your financial goals. Financial professionals can also be helpful with many of the advanced uses of

529 college savings plans that are discussed in Chapter 15, *Taking the Scenic Route: Exploring Advanced Applications of 529 College Savings Plans.*

For some, the desire to begin investing for college can be a catalyst to look for a financial professional to not only help with education planning but to take a broader look at their overall financial picture and goals. This is an opportunity to find someone who fits well with your style and with whom you can feel completely comfortable discussing your current financial situation and exploring your various financial goals and objectives.

If you have an advisor or other financial professional who is already helping you with other investment goals, be sure to mention that you want to begin saving for college for yourself, your child, or a loved one. Your advisor should be familiar with 529 college savings plans and can guide you to a suitable choice for you, given your circumstances and objectives. Financial advice typically comes at a cost. The compensation charged by financial professionals can vary and can be structured as commission-based, fee-based, or some combination thereof. Make certain you inquire about and understand the compensation structure.

Utilizing a Robo-Advisor or 529 Plan Selection App. Digital advice platforms may be a potential solution for those who prefer an approach somewhere between doing it themselves and developing a personal relationship with a financial professional. With some of these advice platforms, a particular state 529 plan and a particular investment option within a plan are recommended based on an investor's responses to a variety of questions.

As some of these platforms may significantly limit their investment recommendations to just one 529 plan or a limited number of 529 plans and even further limit their recommendations to just one or a small number of investment options or approaches within the limited plans they recommend, you'll want to understand upfront how many plans they consider and how their recommendations are made to ensure that a broad enough range of 529 plans and investment options are considered for you given your state of residency and various other aspects of your unique circumstances.

As with any advisory relationship, you'll want to understand how fees are charged and what level of support and advice you'll receive in exchange for the fee and in what form and for what duration. You may be charged a monthly fee or an asset-based fee or some other variation depending on how much you invest or on other factors. You'll also want to determine whether the fee covers ongoing 529 account monitoring and/or advice as your situation, objectives, and/or as market conditions change over time, whether you'll have access to a human advisor should you need additional or personalized support on education planning or other aspects of your financial life, and/or the extent to which you may be on your own once the 529 plan recommendation is made.

There are others who can help too:

Engaging a Financial Counselor. Many communities have financial empowerment and counseling centers with professionals who can assist you at no (or very little) cost. By examining your overall financial picture, reviewing your credit score, helping you to address outstanding debt that you may have, reviewing banking options should you need support in that regard, and/or working with you on the establishment of a budget to help you save for goals including college, financial counselors can play a very valuable role. While they may not be able to give you personalized investment advice, they are likely to be familiar with 529 college savings plans and should be able to help you find the information you need to get started while keeping your overall financial picture in mind.

Consulting with a Tax or Legal Advisor. Tax advisors can be a useful resource when considering 529 college savings plans. Additionally, if you are currently working or plan to be working with an attorney on matters such as trust establishment, estate planning, elder law, marital separation, or divorce, these individuals can help guide you as well.

Regardless of whether you go it alone or work with a financial professional, other professional, or digital advice platform to help guide you, you should be certain to review the offering materials for the 529 college savings plan(s) you are considering. As mentioned earlier, these materials are the official source of information about a particular 529 plan and are sometimes referred to as a program disclosure statement, plan or program description, or as an offering statement, booklet or circular. These materials include important information about investment options, fees and other expenses, tax benefits, risks, other considerations, and rules of the road. They can be obtained through a 529 plan's website, a plan representative, or a financial professional if you are working with one.

Summary. Don't let the decisions of whether to invest directly on your own or to work with a financial professional stand in your way of getting started. Likewise, after you've done your research on various 529 college savings plans, don't let the wide range of investment choices deter you from picking one or more and getting started. You can choose more than one investment option within an account for the same beneficiary, and you can even establish more than one account for the same beneficiary in different 529 college savings plans if you'd like to do so.

Further, you can always change your selection later if you find you would prefer a different 529 plan or investment approach. What's important now is that you just get started!

KEY TAKE-AWAYS

❏   There's no one way to go and you can always switch lanes at a later date.

❏   If you have a trusted advisor, work with that individual. If you are comfortable using information available online and opening an account on your own, do that.

❏   If you later decide on a different approach, you can always open a second account or consider moving assets from your original account to another 529 college savings plan.

❏   What's important is that you get started.

CHAPTER 6

PLANNING YOUR TRIP AND DEVELOPING YOUR ROADMAP: CONSIDERING YOUR TIME HORIZON, RISK TOLERANCE, AND INVESTMENT OBJECTIVES

Whether you are investing on your own or working with a financial professional, after you've selected the 529 college savings plan in which you'd like to invest, you'll need to decide on the particular investment option(s) within the plan that would be suitable for your situation. To do so, you'll need to consider your investment goals, time horizon, and risk tolerance, among other issues, all of which are unique to you. You can do this on your own with the help of tools and resources on 529 plan websites, or with the help of a financial professional.

As an initial step, you'll want to consider the type of higher education your child may pursue (realizing this may be difficult to assess when the child is young), how much that form of education may cost at the time your child will likely pursue it, how much financial aid your child may be eligible to get, and what percentage of the estimated net cost you would like to cover.

Forecast Future Costs. You can look at what the cost of higher learning may be by type of institution (or by actual institutions, if you prefer) when your child will finish high school. There are calculators on many of the 529 college savings plan websites and on other sites that allow you to sort by two-year, four-year, private, in-state public, out-of-state public, etc., and calculators that enable you to estimate what a particular college or university may cost at a specific year in the future. Unless you are certain about the form of higher education your child will pursue or the maximum cost you would be willing to cover, you'll want to keep in mind that the type (and cost) of schooling you'll be saving for may change as your child's interests, aptitudes, and academic and career interests evolve. If you're not at all sure which type of school might be appropriate, you can take an average of several types to get yourself started.

Estimate Financial Aid. There are calculators that can help you to obtain a very rough estimate of the amount of grants your child may be eligible for and what your family's expected contribution (EFC) toward college costs could be. These tools are available on some of the 529 plan websites, through The College Board, and through other sites, to help provide you with estimates. If you are working with a financial professional, that person should be able to assist as well.

Identify the Portion You'd Like to Cover. Decide on the percentage of estimated net costs you'd like to be able to cover. Your goal, for instance, may be to cover 50% of the net cost of a four-year in-state public university education beginning in the year 2035. Remember that whatever percentage you plan to cover, it will make a meaningful difference in the amount your child needs to come up with through working or by borrowing with student loans and repaying with interest.

It's important to keep in mind that if your child winds up receiving a scholarship or attends a military academy and does not need the money you have saved, you may withdraw your money without penalty. You will simply need to pay tax that you had not paid on earnings accrued while the investments were in the account growing tax deferred.

Time Horizon. Identify your time horizon. This is the amount of time your money will be invested. It is the period between your account establishment and when you plan to withdraw funds for their intended use. Some college savers, for instance, plan to withdraw 25% of their account value per year over a four-year period to help pay for college costs. Others may intend to withdraw funds on a different schedule based on other resources or circumstances. The manner in which you plan to spend down your investment needs to be considered as it will affect how long your funds will be invested.

Many investors will calculate their time horizon based on when their beneficiary will likely go to college and the number of years over which the investment will be used to pay for college. Your timeframe for use of your funds is unique to you and you must carefully factor that in.

A note about K–12 use: If, in addition to saving for college, you are planning to make withdrawals from your account to cover elementary or secondary tuition (K–12), your time horizon will be shorter based on that intended use. Your investment strategy will need to reflect the shorter time horizon and the time period over which you will be withdrawing funds. Your proposed spending patterns can affect the type of investment that will be suited for your situation.

Since many of the 529 college savings plan investment portfolios were originally designed for those saving for higher (versus elementary or secondary) education, if you intend to use funds toward elementary or secondary school tuition, you should carefully consider what investment options are available to those saving for K–12 tuition in addition to saving for higher education costs. Information about this should be available on 529 college savings plan websites or within 529 plan offering materials. If you are uncertain about your options and/or if you prefer to have financial advice and guidance versus investing on your own, you should speak with a financial professional to help you determine how best to prepare for both shorter- and longer-term educational goals. You may, for instance, be advised to set up separate 529 accounts with different investment strategies for the two distinctly different purposes. The investment strategies you select need to align with your intended use for the funds and the timing thereof.

Risk Tolerance. In preparing to make your investment selections, it is critical that you consider how comfortable you are with risk and the potential loss of the money you invest. While some 529 college savings plans have one or two fully insured investment options or ones that have very little risk, most of the investment options in most of the 529 college savings plans are subject to market risk, and this can include the possible loss of the money you invest.

Whether working with a financial professional or deciding on your own, it is important to review the 529 college savings plan's offering statement (sometimes referred to as a program disclosure statement, plan or program description, or as an offering statement, booklet, or circular) to gain an understanding of the types of investments that are available, the risk associated with each, the performance history, and other critical information such as fees and expenses. The most current performance information can be found on or through the 529 college savings plan's website. Typically, the riskier the investment option, the greater the potential reward. The smaller the earnings potential, typically the safer and less risky the option. Understanding your comfort with risk and your ability to withstand risk is essential.

Most 529 college savings plans offer investment options that are classified as conservative, moderate, and aggressive, among others, and do a good job of explaining what each means.

In addition to providing you with annualized investment performance over a one-year, five-year, ten-year, and since-inception period in their program offering materials and on their websites as well, investment firms must also provide you with disclosure about potential investment risk. It is important for you to keep in mind that while published performance figures give you a retrospective look at how particular investments performed over specific time periods, **past** performance should never be considered a guarantee of future investment results.

Investment Objective. Your investment objective will help identify the type of investments or investment strategies that will help you reach your financial goal. Your objective is the purpose for your investment expressed in terms of the level of risk and return you are seeking. Many 529 plans have tools on their websites that help you assess your risk tolerance through a series of questions. These assessment tools will help you identify what types of investments would match your comfort with market ups and downs. For instance, these tools may ask you whether potential loss will likely cause you to lose sleep, or whether the opportunity for higher investment returns outweighs the risk of loss. Based on your answers, you will be provided information on types of investments that would align with your stated preferences.

If you are working with a financial professional, that individual can help you choose an appropriate investment option, or mix of investment options, based on a variety of factors including risk, time horizon, and investment goals. Financial professionals can also provide recommendations on when it may be appropriate to make changes, while keeping in mind other financial goals and investments you may have.

Style of Management. With some 529 college savings plans, you'll be given the choice of actively or passively managed investment options or a combination of both. Actively managed funds are run by a portfolio manager or research team which actively aims to beat a particular benchmark by using research, market forecasts, their own expertise, and years of investing experience. Passively managed (or index) funds track a market by owning all, or a representative sample, of the components of an index. Their goal is to match a particular stock or bond market index.

Types of Investment Choices. Below are some high-level descriptions of the types of investment strategies that are typically available through many 529 college savings plans. This is not a detailed review of all options but is intended to give you a sense of some basic categories you are likely to see. 529 plan websites and program materials will provide you with comprehensive details about all available investment options including investment design, historical performance, pricing, and any risks you should consider. Even within the same style of investing, the actual investment portfolios offered by different state 529 college savings plans can vary greatly, so be sure to take a close look at the options within the actual plan that you choose and make sure they align well with your objectives. Many 529 college savings plans allow you to invest in a combination of investment options.

Age-based and enrollment- (or target-) date portfolios. Many 529 college savings plans offer age-based or enrollment-date investment options, which are popular choices among investors. These investment options are designed to gradually become more conservative (and typically, less risky) as the child gets closer to starting college. While the goal is similar, the manner in which risk is reduced over time is different for age-based and enrollment-date investment options. Read the plan materials carefully, contact the plan's call center if you are investing on your own, or speak with an advisor, if you have one, to understand how these and other investment options work.

These portfolios typically begin with investments in equities, then shift over time to fixed income investments and/or cash, short-term reserves, or principal-protected investments. Within age-based or enrollment-date options, investors can often choose the level of risk they prefer. As most age-based options are typically designed with college being the target date, you will want to look at other options for funds you may need sooner, for instance to pay K–12 tuition, as your time horizon will be shorter.

Static investment portfolios. Unlike age-based portfolios, the asset mix in static portfolios does not change as the beneficiary nears college but instead, stays static over time in one or more underlying funds. Examples of static portfolios include target risk and single or individual fund portfolios (described below).

Target risk portfolios. These static portfolios focus on a defined risk level, such as conservative, conservative growth, moderate, moderate growth, aggressive, or other risk levels. Target risk portfolios interest those who wish to align their investments with their comfort level in varying degrees of investment risk.

Single (or individual) fund portfolios. These static portfolios are invested entirely in a single underlying mutual, exchange-traded, or other type of fund. These portfolios interest those who want to create their own customized investment mix through a number of single fund portfolios.

Principal-protected or stable value portfolios. While these portfolios are not fully insured, they seek to produce stable returns higher than a money market fund while avoiding loss of principal. These portfolios interest those who want liquidity and safety for all or a portion of their investment. They may identify what investment return you can expect to receive.

Fully-insured options. Some, but not all, 529 college savings plans offer fully-insured options which are suitable for conservative investors and/or those wishing to preserve all or a portion of their account value as their child grows closer to needing the funds. The return on these investments is typically low. They are desirable for those who prefer safety over investment return.

Typically, the higher the risk, the higher the potential investment return. The lower the risk, the lower the potential investment return. In most 529 college savings plans, you may select more than one investment option. You, together with an advisor, if you have one, decide what percentage of your initial and future contributions should be allocated to each.

Don't Set It and Forget It! Much like getting your car inspected on a periodic basis, you should be checking on your college savings account(s) on a regular basis as well. It is critical that you refrain from taking a set-it-and-forget-it approach. For instance, when your child is getting closer to college, or when you have a better sense of what your child may want to pursue, you may want to adjust the amount you are saving, your investment selections, and/or timeline. If you are saving for more than one child, you will want to review each account separately with each child's unique timeline and circumstances in mind. As stated earlier, when your child is an infant or toddler, you may not know the type of education your child will be inclined to pursue, but as they grow in interests and abilities, you and they may have a better sense. Don't ignore the signs along the road.

Speak to an advisor or other financial professional, if you have access to one, to help guide you regarding any adjustments that need to be made in light of your unique circumstances. If you do not have one, you may contact your 529 plan with any questions you may have. While the call center personnel cannot provide personalized investment advice, they can answer a wide range of questions and point you to information that may be helpful to you.

A Peek into My Journey

When our son was young, to estimate the amount we needed to save, we looked at the potential cost of both private and public 4-year colleges for the year he would enter college (2017) and took an average between the two as we were unsure what type of school he would ultimately pursue. With those costs in mind and a recognition that tuition inflation was growing at nearly twice the rate of general inflation, we decided to invest in an age-based moderate growth portfolio.

We needed the possibility of growth and were comfortable with the amount of risk that was described in the program materials. When our son was about two years away from college, we decided to move a portion of the value of our current investment option to an insured option within the 529 plan because even though the age-based option we had invested in had become more conservative over time, we still wanted to eliminate the risk of even a temporary loss, should there be a market downturn in the final years leading up to college. For us, it was worth foregoing some potential growth on that portion of our investment in exchange for peace of mind.

KEY TAKE-AWAYS

❏ Your financial goals, time horizon, risk tolerance, and investment objectives are all unique to you and are dependent upon your own circumstances.

❏ Carefully consider your comfort with risk by speaking with an advisor if you have one, or by exploring tools on 529 plan websites that help you assess your risk tolerance.

❏ Carefully review details about available investment options on 529 plan websites, third party sites that compare options, or with an advisor, if you have one.

❏ Just as you take your car in for regular inspections, you should revisit your investment selections periodically to make sure they still align with your initial vision and circumstances.

CHAPTER 7

STAYING ON COURSE: INCORPORATING TIPS AND TRICKS TO KEEP ON TRACK AND TO REMIND YOU THAT YOU'RE IN THE DRIVER'S SEAT

Once you have opened your account to save for college, you'll want to stay on track and always remember you are in the driver's seat. Experts in the field of habit-forming behaviors assert that it's what you consistently (not occasionally) do that makes the biggest difference with long-term goals. Let's examine ways to set yourself up for success.

Mindset. Whenever you embark on something new, your frame of mind at the outset can make a big difference in the outcome. Developing the discipline that is needed to design and stick to a plan for long-term goals starts with your mindset. You'll have a much more favorable experience if you think of budgeting and planning as a path to financial freedom for you and your child versus an experience of self-denial. Likewise, if you recognize the fact that your daily actions can very much influence the quality of your family's future, you'll be more successful than if you view aspects of your financial life as being entirely out of your control. Lastly, you'll be more likely to stick with your plan.

Do. Or do not. There is no try."

—Master Yoda, *The Empire Strikes Back*[5]

This quote reminds us that committing to *do* versus committing to *try* has a much greater impact. A commitment to *try to save* has a built-in excuse for failure. Committing *to do* (versus try to do) is much more impactful. Mindset matters.

Share Your Commitment. Sharing with others your goal of saving for your child's future can be beneficial in a number of ways.

• Once you've stated the goal you're working toward, it becomes less abstract and more real. Speaking about it helps you solidify your vision and commitment, and helps you believe in the possibility of achievement.

• Sharing your goal with others increases your accountability. Once others know about it, they may check in to see how you are progressing. While you don't need to go into tremendous detail with everyone you tell about your college savings goal, there is a benefit to sharing more deeply with one or more others and asking them to be your accountability partners.

---

[5] *Star Wars V—The Empire Strikes Back*, Lucasfilm. 1980.

- Letting others know you are saving for your child's educational dreams gives them an opportunity to rally with you and join in your mission. As a dear friend of mine says, "Many hands make light the task."

- Those who love your child will welcome an opportunity to lend a hand. More on this in Chapter 10, *Realizing You Don't Need to Travel Alone: Engaging Others to Join You on Your Journey.*

- You'll be inspiring others to save for the children in their life by sharing the commitment you've undertaken. We often get the best ideas from friends, family, and colleagues. You'll be leading by example and others will thank you for showing them the way.

Revisit Your Budget. Make saving for college a line item in your budget just like you do for other monthly expenses. While it technically isn't an expense, treating it as one will decrease the likelihood that you will view it as optional or as an afterthought.

Break it Down. Let's face it. Some goals can be hard for your mind to grasp and to stick with because of their size and the length of time to reach the goal. It is extremely helpful to break sizeable goals into smaller, more manageable steps which feel less daunting. Completing small tasks consistently like automating your contributions as discussed in the following section, or avoiding unnecessary expenditures each day (as discussed in Chapter 9, *Creating a Travel Budget: Saving More by Spending Less*) will provide you with a sense of accomplishment. Also, periodically checking in on how far you have come and recognizing you are making progress toward something that matters will bring you joy.

"Success is the product of daily habits."

—James Clear, *Atomic Habits*[6]

Automate Your Contributions. After you've decided on how much you can comfortably commit to contributing each week or month and included that figure in your budget, enabling your contributions to become second nature through automation will help you tremendously. Studies show that we're much more likely to pursue and stick with healthy money habits when they're easy.

Nearly all 529 plans can accommodate automatic contributions by way of electronic funds transfer from your savings or checking account or through payroll deduction. Establishing a monthly automatic contribution plan, in which money is directly deposited into the 529 account versus first passing through your hands, will eliminate the guesswork and risk that the money will not be invested. You won't need to continually decide whether and when to contribute, or to remind yourself to do so.

---

[6] Clear, James. *Atomic Habits: An Easy & Proven Way to Build Good Habits & Break Bad Ones*. Avery, October 2018.

Consider Payroll Deduction. While any form of automation will help you with saving, making automatic contributions from your paycheck versus bank account will help you reach your savings goals even faster. According to ISS Market Intelligence, individuals who contribute to 529 plan accounts from their paychecks save on average 75% more than those who contribute from checking or saving.[7]

Engage Your Employer. Ask your employer to help you save for higher education by directing deductions from your paycheck to a 529 college savings plan. There is often little or no cost to your employer for helping facilitate this, and some employers may even be willing to match a portion of your contributions as an added benefit! Employers can play a significant role in helping employees and their families not only learn about 529 college savings plans, but also save for higher education through them.

Watch Your Expenditures. Keep an eye out each day for expenses that you can reduce or eliminate. For those unnecessary but enjoyable expenditures that are important for you to keep, consider a trade-off with something that's less important to you. If you make it a point each day to reduce your expenditures even slightly, you'll be well on your way. More on the impact of slight adjustments in expenditures in Chapter 9, *Creating a Travel Budget: Saving More by Spending Less and Incorporating Minimalism.*

---

[7] ISS Market Intelligence 529 Data Industry Analysis, May 2019.

Pay Down Your Debt. Get in the habit of avoiding the accumulation of debt and paying down whatever debt you have as quickly as possible. Taking intentional steps to get yourself out of debt will help you to save more and help you and/or your child avoid having to take out sizeable loans.

Put College on your Wish List. Making contributions to your child's 529 college savings plan a part of the family celebrations as a new gift-giving tradition is an excellent habit to develop and maintain. Gift givers will thank you for the smart and easy gift idea. More on this in Chapter 10, *Realizing You Don't Need to Travel Alone: Engaging Others to Join You on Your Journey.*

Apply Extra Money. Putting unexpected money that you receive into your 529 college savings account is another good idea. For instance, every time you receive a tax refund, some additional compensation, or a bonus, place that money or a portion of it in your child's account. Some parents take all or part of any raise in income and apply it directly to their 529 account. If you happen to inherit money, placing some of your inheritance in a 529 account may be a fitting way to honor the memory of your loved one.

Maximize Money from Milestones. For many parents, getting your child out of diapers can result not only in a huge sense of accomplishment but also in a cost savings that can be immediately applied to your college savings account. In fact, for parents who had been spending $60 a month on average on diapers, wipes, and creams, more than $16,000 can be saved over 15 years assuming a

5% annual rate of return. Likewise, for some families, having your child enter kindergarten can result in the elimination of daycare costs which can also be applied to college savings.

Additionally, for stay-at-home parents who left the workplace while raising young children, having your child (or youngest child) enter kindergarten may free you to seek or resume paid employment. Extra earnings can provide more money for long-term goals like retirement and college.

15 YEARS OF NO-DIAPERS
yields a savings of
OVER $16,000!

Assumptions:
Diaper savings of
$60/month invested
from age 3 to 18 at
a 5% rate of return.

Review Your Progress. Make it a point to review your progress at least twice a year. Keeping an eye on how you're doing is valuable for a number of reasons. When you witness and celebrate the progress you are making, you are more likely to stick with it. Additionally, it gives you a chance to make certain that your initial objectives and preferences are still the same. It also gives you a chance to make adjustments based on your progress toward your goals. Perhaps you can make this part of back-to-school season when your child is one year closer to college and/or when your child brings home a report card. Alternatively, you can decide on other logical times during each year to take an honest look at how your investments have performed, as well as your progress. If you are working with a financial professional, it's likely you will have at least one review annually of your total financial picture. If you are investing directly with a 529 plan, check with your plan to see what tools they have to help you to assess your progress.

With many investors opting for receipt of electronic statements online versus paper statements in the mail, sometimes accounts become both out of sight and out of mind. It may benefit you to request paper statements at least once a year. Many 529 plans give you the option to have a year-end statement sent in paper form even if you are signed up for electronic delivery throughout the year.

Create a Vision/Promise Board. We talked about finding your *Why* and your vision for the future in Chapter 1, *Start with your Destination in Mind: Embracing Your Why as You Begin Your Savings*

Journey. One idea is to place one or more symbols of that vision on a physical or mental vision board. Your vision board could include the future you are aiming for, and also one or more symbols that remind you of the promises you made to yourself in order to fulfill that vision for the future. Envisioning the future that you want for you and your child can be a helpful motivation. If you can *see* it, you have a greater chance of believing it and achieving it.

VISION/PROMISE
BOARD

Stories from the Road

In terms of visual reminders, one parent told me she posted her student loan payoff letter in a visible location as a reminder of what she wanted to avoid for her children. Another took pictures of her two children in tee shirts from her alma mater. Yet another posted the words *Financial Freedom* with some pictures on her wall.

Another couple mentioned that they created a vision board as they were preparing to marry and included on it pictures of the type of life they would like to have as a married couple. Their vision board included the type of house they would like to live in, the number of children that they'd like to have, and pictures of schools their children could attend. They firmly attribute the life they now have to the vision of it they created years prior.

In terms of putting "unexpected money" to good use, a friend named Jennifer inherited $45,000 from her grandfather when her children were 9, 7 and 2 years of age. At the time, she and her husband had trouble deciding how best to put the money to use with so many competing expenses and needs. There were bills to pay off, ongoing daycare expenses to address, a new car that would have been helpful and retirement plans to contribute to. And of course, there were "nice-to-haves" like a vacation or home improvements to consider as well.

Instead, she and her husband decided to divide the money equally and to place $15,000 for each child in their state's 529 plan. Years later, Jennifer can't say enough about how happy she is to have selected the 529 plan over other all options for the inherited funds. She is thrilled to have honored her grandfather's memory by substantially covering her children's higher education expenses. She is so relieved to know that her children can start off their adult lives without the burden of student loan debt she once had and she knows how proud her grandfather would be to have funded his great-grandchildren's futures thanks to the generous gift he left to her.

A Peek into My Journey

As soon as I returned to work after maternity leave, I made a commitment to contribute automatically to my 529 account from my bi-weekly earnings. I knew there'd be little income left to spare with the many new costs associated with having a child, but I figured if money was automatically withdrawn from my pay and deposited into my college savings account, it would somehow be easier. Between juggling work and motherhood, anything else added to my plate needed to be easy to stick with. And it was.

While I opted for electronic statements to cut down on mail, I did request that year-end statements be sent to me by mail. That way I was sure to see them, could check on our progress, and review the paper statement with our son in age-appropriate ways as he grew up.

KEY TAKE-AWAYS

❏ Mindset matters. Adjust your mindset to incorporate the freedom that planning will offer you and your child in the future. And call upon your inner Yoda to help you be relentless in doing what you need to do versus simply *trying* to do it.

❏ Create a Vision/Promise Board that contains symbols representing both your vision for your child's future and the promises you made to get them there. Seeing is believing—and will help get you there.

❏ Set yourself up for success by arranging to contribute automatically, either directly from your saving or checking account or even better, from your pay. Don't leave anything to chance.

❏ Tell others about the college savings goal you set and enable friends and family to rally around you. Remember that sharing your goal may help others to learn about 529 plans and begin saving for the children in their lives as well.

CHAPTER 8

REACHING A FORK IN THE ROAD: DECIDING WHICH WAY TO GO WHEN FACED WITH CONFLICTING PRIORITIES

There will be points in your journey when you may not know which direction to go, or where to go first when faced with multiple priorities. These are two financial priorities that are discussed most by personal finance experts:

Emergency Funds. Personal finance professionals strongly recommend that you have funds earmarked for an emergency in a form that is easy to access. Nearly all agree that putting at least $1,000 into an emergency fund in a liquid account and then, growing that initial amount to the equivalent of three, six, or even nine months of living expenses should take precedence over every other financial goal.

Retirement Savings. For most parents, putting your own needs before your child(ren)'s is not a familiar concept. Personal finance professionals, however, strongly recommend that when it comes to choosing between retirement and college savings, retirement savings should come first. One popular analogy offered to parents is to follow the advice given to airplane passengers regarding the potential loss of cabin pressure. Personal finance professionals strongly advise that putting on one's own oxygen mask first (saving for retirement) should take a priority over assisting a child with a mask (saving for college). After all, while students can apply for financial aid for college, there is none available for retirement.

Most agree that saving for retirement at least to the level to avail yourself of any employer matching contributions should be a priority. Others recommend that once you are consistently saving around 12–15% of your salary for retirement, you can begin making regular contributions to college savings accounts as well. Preparing to fund higher education is widely regarded by investors as the second most important savings need after retirement.

The reality is that saving for retirement versus college is not an either/or situation, as the two can impact each other significantly. While the argument is correct that you cannot borrow or obtain financial aid for retirement as you can for college, the failure to plan adequately for college expenses can become a retirement problem. Parents sometimes wind up borrowing from their retirement accounts, sometimes with a penalty, to send children to college. They also wind up borrowing from the equity in their homes which then needs to be repaid. Or they end up taking out loans on behalf of their children, then must work well into their retirement years to pay them back.

Failing to plan for college costs can jeopardize long-term financial security of the entire family, as can failing to save for retirement. The two topics are interconnected. Parents who become unable to support themselves in their later years because they did not adequately save for retirement can become reliant on their adult children for support. Likewise, children who graduate with an enormous amount of educational debt due to failure to save in advance, often remain reliant on their parents for support because they are unable to launch into a more independent adult life.

In terms of how to successfully save for both retirement and college, my thoughts are two-fold:

1. Open a college savings account as soon as possible, even if you are not yet in a position to contribute regularly. That way, friends and family can immediately begin to contribute for birthdays, holidays, and other special occasions. You can contribute when you have extra money (like a tax refund or other windfall). Additionally, if you work for an employer who is willing to contribute toward your college savings, having an account established can help you to avail yourself of that benefit. You will learn in Chapter 10, *Realizing You Don't Need to Travel Alone: Engaging Others to Join You on Your Journey* just how easy it is for others to contribute once you have your account established.

2. Take a very honest look at your income and expenditures to identify if there's room to increase earnings or reduce spending. As you'll learn in Chapter 9, *Creating a Travel Budget: Saving More by Spending Less and Incorporating Minimalism*, spending less can have a significant impact on how much you have to save. Eliminating unnecessary expenditures and developing and sticking to a financial plan can help increase your chances of effectively saving for both

retirement and education. And of course, increasing your earnings through advancement in your current career or by taking on a side hustle can certainly help as well.

Stories from the Road

In order to both save for retirement and fund their children's college savings accounts, a family I know decided to sell their home and downsize to a more affordable home in their same neighborhood. By reducing their expenses by over $1,500/month, they successfully contributed to both retirement and college savings accounts.

In another example, a couple in Washington State made a decision to keep their aging minivan for several more years to avoid a $480 monthly car payment for a new vehicle. Instead of making a monthly payment over three years for a vehicle they really didn't need, they invested for the future what they would have otherwise spent. This strategy resulted in additional account contributions of over $17,000.

KEY TAKE-AWAYS

❑ Most personal finance professionals agree that neither the establishment of an emergency fund nor the consistent funding of a retirement account should take a back seat to college savings.

❑ After your emergency fund is in place, experts suggest developing the practice of funding your retirement account at least up to your employer's matching contribution before beginning to fund your college savings accounts.

❑ Open a 529 account, even if you are not yet ready to contribute on a regular basis, so that others can begin to contribute if they wish to. If you wait until you are completely ready, you may lose valuable time and even worse, you may never get started.

CHAPTER 9

CREATING A TRAVEL BUDGET:
SAVING MORE BY SPENDING LESS AND
INCORPORATING MINIMALISM

It's easy to overlook the fact that one of the best ways to help you to save is to take a careful look at what you spend. Start with a review of your fixed monthly expenses, and then document and carefully review what you are spending on an ad hoc basis. It's amazing what you will find if you make a note of everything you spend over the course of a week or month. If you think intentionally about what expenditures are essential and which are "nice to have" and then make some adjustments, you'll have more money to place in your college savings account.

In terms of areas in which you can make some adjustments, you may want to think about ongoing expenditures that you might be overlooking such as subscriptions, memberships, or paid apps that you once signed up for but are no longer using. Further, you may want to consider re-examining your cable bill to see if you're being billed for channels you truly enjoy or whether there are extras that can be eliminated for cost savings. Also, personal finance experts recommend checking periodically on car or home insurance rates to see if you are getting the lowest rates for your needs and doing the same with mobile phone and internet services. You may not need to switch providers to get more preferable rates.

Sometimes simply letting your provider know that you are looking around for lower rates can result in the provider making an offer to reduce your current costs.

Reducing everyday expenditures even slightly can lead to big savings. For instance, when expenditures are lowered and savings are invested monthly over 18 years with an estimated 5 percent annual rate of return:

- Cutting costs by $1.00 a day can yield approximately $10,476

- Cutting costs by $2.50 a day can yield $26,190

- Cutting costs by $5.00 a day can yield $52,380

Cutting larger fixed expenses (like cable, insurance, or mobile phone bills) can add even more substantially to your savings.

Think about what you may be able to reduce or eliminate in your current budget or trim from your daily miscellaneous spending. Make note of those expenses.

DAILY SAVINGS CAN **ADD UP**

JUST $1 A DAY

Total Savings From Birth.............$10,476.06
Total Savings From Age 3.............$8,018.67
Total Savings From Age 5.............$6,573.28
Total Savings From Age 10..........$3,532.22
Total Savings From Age 15...........$1,162.60

JUST $2 50 A DAY

Total Savings From Birth.............$26,190.15
Total Savings From Age 3...........$20,046.67
Total Savings From Age 5...........$16,433.20
Total Savings From Age 10...........$8,830.54
Total Savings From Age 15...........$2,906.50

JUST $5 A DAY

Total Savings From Birth.............$52,380.30
Total Savings From Age 3...........$40,093.34
Total Savings From Age 5...........$32,866.41
Total Savings From Age 10.........$17,661.08
Total Savings From Age 15...........$5,813.00

JUST $10 A DAY

Total Savings From Birth...........$104,760.61
Total Savings From Age 3...........$80,186.68
Total Savings From Age 5...........$65,732.82
Total Savings From Age 10.........$35,322.15
Total Savings From Age 15.........$11,626.00

Assumptions: 5% rate of return compounded monthly until age 18

EXPENDITURES
TO REDUCE, ELIMINATE,
OR RECONSIDER

In terms of spending less, it's valuable for your family to come up with activities and traditions that don't involve money. Taking walks together after dinner, playing board games, exploring the great outdoors near your home, volunteering together as a family, and so on can all create great memories and demonstrate that money is not needed to have fun.

Unplanned Purchases. As parents, we sometimes let emotion (versus reason) control purchasing decisions, especially when they are spur of the moment. Step back, when possible, to determine if your purchase is really necessary. Consider whether you will need that item as much tomorrow as you think you do today. These are great opportunities to discuss needs versus wants with your child(ren).

Shopping and other Rewards Programs. When you do spend, remember you are in the driver's seat. Be sure to spend thoughtfully and if you use credit cards, be sure to pay them off in full each month to avoid finance charges. Also, check to see if any of your expenditures can be linked to programs that provide cash back for college. There are rewards programs, including a popular one called Upromise, that enable a percentage of every dollar spent to be directed to a college savings account. Whether you're shopping for everyday items or making a larger ticket purchase, receiving even a small percentage back for your college savings objectives can be helpful. With some programs, friends and family may also be able to have their shopping rewards contributed to your child's college savings account. Additionally, if you happen to still have student loans of your own that you are repaying, some shopping rewards programs even enable you to direct a percentage of your purchases to pay down student loan debt.

Reconsider Housing and Cars. The most significant expenses for most families are their home and cars. Think critically about whether the fixed expenses for your home and car(s) will enable you to realize the financial goals you have for your child(ren)'s future. If you feel you may be sacrificing peace of mind in exchange for your current lifestyle, you may want to consider some adjustments.

The Role Minimalism Can Play. What is minimalism? Minimalism is an approach to living that can assist you in finding freedom from the trappings of the consumer culture we've built our lives around. The more belongings we have in our life, the more costly and complicated it can be. There is a tremendous joy that can come from living with less. In addition to the peace of mind that comes from a less cluttered home and fewer possessions to keep track of and maintain, it's likely that you'll have more available resources to save toward college and more time to spend with your children exploring their interests, talents, and values, as well as how they relate to the academic and career options they may want to consider. It takes time and focus to have these discussions, and to listen without judgment and interruption. Being truly present is a priceless gift you can give your children, and fewer distractions can lead to deeper connections.

Further, there's a real value in raising a child who is less of a consumer and who learns that personal belongings are not the key to happiness.

Additionally, it's also possible that by purchasing less, you will create less waste and thereby, help the environment. Joshua Becker, author of *The More of Less*[8] and *The Minimalist Home*,[9] writes about the impact the principles of minimalism he and his wife embraced have had on his children. Among the lessons his children have learned are that they don't need to buy things to be happy and that they don't need to live life like everyone else. He says they've also learned to think carefully about their purchases and to share gladly with others.

The example you set can help your children develop into financially responsible and more resourceful adults. Children's eyes are wide open and they learn from you every day.

Stories from the Road

A family I know made a decision to limit vacations to every three years and to incorporate some enjoyable staycations during the other years. They found that staying close to home afforded them the opportunity to tackle some home projects together as a family and to explore aspects of the area in which they lived that they would have otherwise not gotten acquainted with had they traveled out of town. Their children got involved in deciding on the home projects and local areas to visit. They also found that they looked forward to and

[8] Becker, Joshua. *The More of Less: Finding the Life You Want Under Everything You Own.* WaterBrook, May 2016.
[9] Becker, Joshua. *The Minimalist Home: A Room-by-Room Guide to a Decluttered, Refocused Life.* WaterBrook, 1st Edition December 2018.

enjoyed their out-of-town vacations more when they didn't take them as frequently.

A Peek into My Journey

While I do regret some of my purchases and financial decisions through the years, we did take time to periodically review our expenditures and adjust in meaningful ways. For instance, when our son was in middle school, we took a careful look at our household budget with him and it was he who suggested we eliminate our cable service. That alone saved us $2,000/year which we were able to instead direct to his college savings account.

Additionally, we made a decision as a family to drive the same automobile for nearly 21 years. In light of this, both literally and figuratively, that car has helped get our son to college—it has literally transported him there and back and by not purchasing a new automobile throughout our son's life, the money we saved by not spending on a newer automobile helped us save more for college.

Lastly, we've incorporated minimalism into our life by downsizing to a smaller home and getting rid of many unnecessary belongings. By owning less, we have found that it's much easier to see and appreciate the belongings we have, and we spend far less time looking for misplaced items. Life is so much more relaxing with fewer belongings to maintain. We have found freedom through simplicity.

KEY TAKE-AWAYS

❑ How much you will be able to save in the long run has a lot to do with how much you spend.

❑ Pursuing family activities that don't involve cost can be some of the most rewarding and memorable.

❑ Taking an honest look at current expenditures and cutting back where you can will free up additional money that can be deposited to your child's college savings account.

❑ Stepping away for a few minutes and catching yourself when you are about to let emotion drive your buying decisions can be helpful.

❑ Establishing a lifestyle with fewer belongings can pay off in more ways than you can imagine. There are priceless lessons for your child in this as well, which can pay off for years (and generations) to come.

Chapter 10

Realizing You Don't Need to Travel Alone: Engaging Others to Join You on Your Journey

One of the many benefits of 529 college savings plans is that once you open your account, you can immediately begin to invite others to contribute too.

The Power of Gifting Tools. Many 529 plans have easy-to-use gifting tools for account owners to invite others to contribute to their accounts. In fact, some 529 college savings plans enable you to sign up to use the gifting tool as soon as your account is established. The gifting features enable account owners to invite friends and family to contribute to their accounts by sharing a bar code or an electronic or printed deposit coupon with friends and family so they can make one-time or periodic contributions. Be sure to find out whether the plan you are invested in or are considering has this type of feature and learn how to use it. Gift givers in your life will welcome an easy way to invest in your child's future.

Beyond gifting tools associated with particular 529 college savings programs, there are also independent gifting platforms that work with most any 529 college savings or 529A (ABLE) plan. One such example is GiftofCollege.com, where 529 account owners can create shareable profiles through which gifts can be made to their 529 accounts. (In full disclosure: I am employed by Gift of College, Inc.) The shareable profile enables friends, family, and even employers to contribute. Gift of College also has gift cards available online and at major retailers that can be given and redeemed into most any 529 college savings or ABLE account. Gift cards are particularly useful when the gift giver doesn't want to spoil the surprise by asking the 529 account owner for an invitation or deposit coupon in order to contribute. They're also great gifts for persons who need (or will soon need) to open a 529 college savings account but have not yet done so—for instance, as a baby shower gift. The gift card is a great reminder to get started and can serve as the very first contribution. There are other commercial gift giving platforms as well that you can explore if you care to use something in addition to the gifting features your 529 plan offers.

Make it a Tradition. Once you have opened a 529 college savings account, it becomes very easy to incorporate saving into yearly celebrations and to invite others to invest, one occasion at a time. It's no surprise that those who love your child(ren) will naturally want to give gifts in honor not only of their arrival but for holidays, birthdays, and other milestones through the years. While some may look to you for suggestions and sizes, others will struggle on their own for "just the right gift" and may worry that it's something that your child already has, that won't fit, or that they won't like. You can help alleviate this stress.

Make it Easy. I suspect that at least some, if not all, of your friends and family would welcome a suggestion of a gift that's easy to give, and saving for college is something everyone can feel good about for years to come. You can make this simpler for everyone involved by thanking them for the thoughtful gifts they've already given while suggesting a contribution to your child's college savings account instead going forward. If they feel they still want to give something "tangible," suggest a much smaller gift (like a book or small toy), a hand-written letter, or something homemade. You could say something along the lines of: *"As a family, we're making a conscious effort to cut back on toys, clothing, and other material belongings and instead, are letting loved ones know that we are making it a priority to save for college for the kids. If you're wondering what to buy this holiday season, we'd welcome a contribution to their college accounts. Enclosed is the information you will need."*

It's a Win/Win/Win. Most people will likely prefer to not spend time shopping for your child and guessing on sizes, preferences, and what the child may already have. Suggesting a contribution to the college savings account is a win/win/win. The gift giver wins by being given a smart and easy gift idea and wins by avoiding hours of shopping and the potential of buyer's remorse. You win by not having to deal with duplicate gifts or wrongly sized items that need to be returned or the clutter associated with plastic toys, electronic games, stuffed animals, and pieces of clothing not needed and soon placed in the back of the closet, in the garage or attic. Most importantly, your child(ren) win by having more people interested in their academic future and more funds to pursue whatever form of education they desire when the time comes.

You'll Be Thanked. Gift givers will thank you for providing an easy-to-give alternative that everyone can feel good about. Your child(ren) will thank you as well someday when student loan debt is minimized or avoided as a result of your circle of friends and family lending a hand.

Get the Conversation Going. Furthermore, unlike more traditional gifts of clothing or toys, gifts toward education provide an opportunity for follow up. As friends and family invest in your child(ren)'s future, it opens the door to priceless conversations through the years about what the future may hold. A contribution toward a college savings account can prompt insightful conversations about what impact a child wants to have on the world after high school and what type of education would be helpful to accomplish those goals. Imagine how good it can feel for loved ones to be a part of something so important. Those who contribute are presented with an opportunity to become a part of the child's dreams.

Break it Down to Build it Up. If you break down the number of celebrations over the years, you'll be surprised by the countless opportunities for others to make a significant impact on your child(ren)'s future. In fact, if you simply count birthdays (18) and one annual holiday (18) each year, you'll have 36 gift-giving occasions before your child reaches adulthood. If just ten close friends and family members give $25 toward your child's 529 account on each occasion in lieu of, or to complement, a smaller more traditional gift, your child could have over $14,000 by the time college rolls around, assuming an estimated annual 5% rate of return. If $50 were given by a total of ten close friends or family members, your child could have over $28,000, and so on.

Add in pre-school, kindergarten, middle school, and high school graduations along with religious celebrations, performances, sporting events, awards, and other milestones, and you're sure to have countless more occasions to celebrate. Plus, it's very likely, many loved ones who join in these celebrations would welcome the opportunity to invest in your child's future with a gift toward college. Gifts from others can really supplement your savings.

Creating a tradition of putting college on your holiday wish list is something that everyone can feel good about. Your friends and family will likely love the idea of rallying together to help your child(ren) graduate with brighter financial outcomes.

Engage your Employer. Lastly, it's a good idea to let your employer know that you are saving for your child's future and that, to make it easier, you would welcome the opportunity to send money to your 529 plan account by way of payroll deduction. You can also ask if your employer may want to consider making a contribution to your account or matching a percentage of the contributions you make as an employee benefit.

Make a List and Check it Twice. Make a list of occasions to incorporate gifting and make a list of individuals who may welcome the opportunity to take the guesswork out of what to buy for holidays and birthdays. You'll be surprised by the number of occasions and gift givers that will come to mind.

CELEBRATIONS

GIFT **GIVERS**

BIRTHDAY & HOLIDAY
GIFT GIVING

■ 5 Gift Givers   ■ 10 Gift Givers

Each Giving Two Gifts Per Year

Twice Annual Gift Amount

$0K $10K $20K $30K $40K $50K $60K

$25
- $7,199.63
- $14,399.26

$50
- $14,399.26
- $28,798.51

$100
- $28,798.51
- $57,597.02

Assumptions: Deposit of gifts every six months.
5% rate of return compounded monthly over 18 years.

Stories from the Road

My friend's daughter and son-in-law include an easy-to-use link for contributions to their sons' college savings accounts in every birthday party invitation. They simply make the following request: *"In lieu of gifts, please consider contributing a few bucks to the boys' college savings account. They truly have everything else they need thanks to the generosity of their grandparents."* The boys' mother reports that almost 90% of the party invitees make a contribution and many thank her for the smart idea. In addition, some party guests choose to bring a small gift from a dollar or inexpensive store so the child has something to unwrap.

A Peek into My Journey

By the time my son was two years old, we realized we had far too many toys, games, stuffed animals and clothing—much of which had been quickly outgrown in terms of size and interest. Family and friends truly had the best of intentions with the purchases they made for birthdays and other special occasions. In retrospect, I wish I had mentioned sooner that he really didn't need another item and that instead, it would be greatly appreciated if gift givers made a contribution of any amount to his college savings account. After all, even a $25 contribution could be applied to books and supplies needed for college someday. By middle school, we did mention our preference and a number of individuals began giving smaller tangible gifts and began making a deposit into our son's account in addition to or instead of what they would have typically given as a gift. These contributions really made a difference.

KEY TAKE-AWAYS

❑ There will be countless occasions in your child's life when others will want to celebrate. These include birthdays, holidays, religious or academic milestones, extra-curricular achievements, and so on.

❑ A wide range of not-so-useful gifts will quite likely be purchased with the best of intentions. Many of these items will be quickly outgrown and your home will become cluttered.

❑ Suggesting an easy-to-give contribution toward higher education may be a welcomed alternative for gift givers and may open the door to meaningful conversations with your child about future aspirations.

❑ Mark your calendar for November to tell friends and family about your wishes for year-end holiday gifts. Mark your calendar for one month prior to your child's birthday to get the word out (or as a reminder to include a note in party invitations) that a contribution to the college account is preferred over other gifts.

❑ Make college savings a go-to gift.

CHAPTER 11

ENCOUNTERING DETOURS AND BUMPS IN THE ROAD: HOW PLANNING AHEAD CAN HELP WITH LIFE'S TWISTS AND TURNS

Let's face it. There's no doubt you may experience some unexpected twists and turns or bumps in the road during your savings journey. As with driving, we sometimes encounter road closures, inclement weather, a sudden need for car repair, or even distracted drivers. Keeping an eye on the weather forecast, planning ahead for your travels, buckling up, and keeping your eyes on the road will help enable you to safely move through unexpected conditions without completely going off course.

Making sure you have emergency savings in place, as well as making sure you have a plan for both retirement and higher education funding underway, will help tremendously as you weather a wide range of road conditions. Additionally, making sure you are living within your means and not overwhelmed or distracted by a larger-than-necessary lifestyle under a pile of possessions will serve you well when you need clarity to address life's inevitable storms.

What could possibly distract you from the well-intentioned plans you made to save for higher education? While there are countless scenarios that can cause financial shocks, below are a few to consider. Each will remind you why starting as early as possible to develop a plan to save for higher education will be beneficial no matter what travel conditions you encounter along the way.

Aging Parents. As part of the "sandwich generation," being a caregiver of both children and an aging family member has become increasingly common and can come with added emotional and financial expense. The need to step in and assist an aging relative sometimes develops unexpectedly and can cause you or your partner to step away from income-producing activities in order to physically lend a hand or can cause you to pay and oversee others to do so.

Work Disruptions. Change in career, job loss, or reduction in pay can interfere with the best-laid plans to save and pay for long-term goals.

Death or Disability of a Partner or Loved One. Loss of income due to death or disability can have a significant impact on savings goals.

Change in Relationship Status. Even the most loving relationships can change over time. Having a plan in place for your children will serve you well whether together or apart. See information on 529 plans and divorce in Chapter 13, *Keeping Your Eyes on the Road: Risks & Special Considerations.*

Economic Shocks. Unexpected household, auto, tax, or medical expenses can throw families off track. Having emergency funds can help you weather these circumstances.

Market Volatility. Making sure you've carefully examined your risk tolerance, time horizon, and investment objectives when you open your various investment accounts, and periodically revisiting them along the way will help with any sudden swings. As your child nears the time during which the funds will be used, you may, for example, wish to consider placing a portion of your funds in more conservative investments depending on the investments the funds are currently in. Age- or target-date options adjust as college nears, however, it's always a good idea to make certain you understand the investments you are currently in and whether any adjustments may be in order depending on your circumstances.

Truly, the future is unpredictable but focusing on what you can control can help make a favorable difference even in unfavorable circumstances. You'll be in a better position to weather life's twists and turns if you have a financial plan in place that includes emergency funds as well as college and retirement savings.

Stories from the Road

A few years back, I met a father whose daughter was overjoyed with having gotten into her dream school after having been waitlisted. Nine months prior, he had unexpectedly lost a job that he had for over 15 years and he was still unemployed. With no college savings account for his daughter and few other savings left to rely on, he had to tell his daughter that she could not attend the school she had worked so hard to get into because the net cost was simply too high. He told me he wished he had saved for college over the years leading up to this time, instead of assuming that he would always be gainfully employed and able to pay when the time came.

As a different example, at the recommendation of a financial advisor, my friend Eileen and her husband began saving for college when their two children were toddlers. When the children were in elementary school, her husband passed away. Because she and her husband had begun saving when the kids were very young by making short-term sacrifices for long-term goals, Eileen had the comfort of knowing that there was a foundation already laid for the children's futures upon which she could continue to build. From the children's perspectives, knowing there was a plan in place to help them pursue their academic and career interests was reassuring and gave them a positive outlook on the future. Knowing that their dad helped set up their plans meant a tremendous amount as well.

A Peek into My Journey

I could not have possibly imagined how the world in general and various circumstances in particular would change between the year 2000 and now, but I did imagine that the costs of college would continue to rise and that my desire to help as much as possible with those costs would continue to be strong. No matter what arose, I continued to save and invest for the future.

I lived through 9/11 as an employee at the World Trade Center complex, the market corrections of 2000 and 2008, and many other unexpected experiences during my journey to save for college. In my son's last year of high school, my mom's health began to decline. As a result, I then had increased financial responsibilities for her and after she passed away, increased responsibilities for my brother who has a developmental disability. All in the same year, my firm exited the line of business that was my focus and my job was eliminated. Fortunately, I had planned ahead for my son's college education which was only one year away. As a result, my son was able to pursue his college dreams without any additional stress on our household finances.

KEY TAKE-AWAYS

❑ You cannot predict what tomorrow will hold, but you can control what you do TODAY to prepare.

❑ Planning today will help you be well-prepared for any road conditions you may encounter on your journey.

CHAPTER 12

CONSIDERING ALTERNATE ROUTES: A LOOK AT OTHER WAYS TO SAVE

In terms of alternative or complementary ways to save, it's important to note that there's no one way to save or invest for the cost of higher education. 529 college savings plans, however, are among the most popular and tax-favored approaches. There are other options that families utilize to prepare for college costs and some families employ a number of different approaches. Below is some general information about several of the approaches that parents consider. Whatever savings or investing vehicles you are considering, it's a good idea to review program offering materials carefully and to speak with a trusted advisor if you have one, or a financial institution's call center to pose any questions you may have.

The following issues should be considered with respect to any savings or investing vehicle:

- Whether there are income, age, or other restrictions
- Minimum and maximum amounts you can invest annually and over the life of the account
- Who controls the account once the future student reaches legal age (18 or 21, depending on your state of residency)
- Whether you can change the beneficiary on the account
- Whether you can revoke gifts made to the account

- Financial aid impact while in the account and following withdrawal
- Fees, expenses, commissions
- Any restrictions on use of funds, penalties, or other limitations
- Federal and state tax treatment when contributed, while invested, and when withdrawn
- Risks
- Earnings potential

Prepaid Tuition Plans. Prepaid Tuition Plans allow account owners to pre-purchase future tuition at a predetermined rate today on a future student's behalf. Account owners pay for future tuition (by years, credits, or units) in one lump sum or over time through installment payments. Some parents and grandparents prefer the certainty of entering a contract to purchase a specific portion of a child's tuition upfront versus investing in a 529 college savings plan and not knowing what the account value will be, due to market fluctuations, and what it will cover in terms of educational costs in the future.

At the time of publication, there are 10 prepaid tuition plan options in existence which are offered by 9 states and by the Private College 529 Plan. The states that have prepaid options are Florida, Maryland, Massachusetts, Michigan, Mississippi, Nevada, Pennsylvania, Texas, and Washington. An additional state, Virginia, is in the process of offering one.

If you live in one of these states, you will want to include the prepaid option in your research. Since each state that has a prepaid tuition plan also has a 529 college savings plan, you can compare the two and consider how they differ and how they could work together as a potential solution for your family's college planning needs.

There is another prepaid tuition plan option to consider. The Private College 529 Plan is a national prepaid tuition plan that provides an opportunity to prepay undergraduate tuition for a beneficiary at approximately 300 participating colleges and universities in the United States regardless of where you live. If you're inclined to send your child(ren) to one or more of the participating private college or universities, you will want to include this plan in your research to learn more about how it works.

Like 529 college savings plans, the 529 prepaid tuition plans are federally tax-advantaged and in some cases have state tax benefits as well. Unlike 529 college savings plans, 529 prepaid tuition plans typically cover only tuition and mandatory fees and most cannot be used toward room and board, books, supplies, and other expenses including K–12 tuition for which 529 college savings plans can be used. There are exceptions. For instance, in Florida, in addition to an option to prepay for tuition and mandatory fees, there is an option to prepay for dormitory expenses.

Some families choose to participate in a prepaid tuition plan and a college savings plan so that they can have money set aside to cover a broad range of anticipated expenses.

Unlike 529 college savings plans, many prepaid tuition plans have residency restrictions for account owners and/or beneficiaries, age requirements for beneficiaries, and time limits for use of funds. Again, there are exceptions. The Massachusetts plan and the Private College 529 Plan, for instance, do not have residency requirements.

Prepaid plans have a defined universe of participating colleges and universities. You will want to understand the various refund or other options available to you should your child decide not to attend a participating school.

As each plan is unique, it is important to obtain specific information directly from plan documents or representatives. The Massachusetts prepaid option, for example, is not a 529 plan but has some similarities. In addition to contacting plans directly, you may also want to visit www.collegesavings.org (the College Savings Plans Network) or www.savingforcollege.com for current and additional information on prepaid tuition plans and to compare 529 plans. Most of the prepaid tuition plans have specific enrollment periods and pricing is typically adjusted annually. Whether the plans are guaranteed, and the extent to which they are, varies as well. Make sure you understand the benefits and risks associated with any option you are considering. Read the program offering materials and talk to a plan representative to make certain you understand exactly how the plans work.

529A (ABLE) Plans. An ABLE plan provides certain individuals with disabilities a tax-advantaged way to save or invest for education as well as a broad range of disability-related expenses without having a negative impact on the person's eligibility for public benefits, such as Medicaid. The annual contribution limit for an ABLE account is currently $15,000 per individual, although working account owners may contribute an additional amount equal to the total of their wages or the poverty limit, whichever is less, provided they are not participating in their employer's retirement plan. Lifetime contribution limits vary by state as do investment options, other features, fees, and expenses.

The National Association of State Treasurers (www.nast.org/able/) along with The ABLE National Resource Center (www.ablenrc.org) managed by the National Disability Institute, are good sources of current information about ABLE plans including how to get started with opening an account. They provide details of the various ABLE programs that are available by state. Be sure to read the program offering materials for rules about who can enroll, how the plans work, and to review information about cost and special considerations. While individuals can generally open an account with any ABLE plan that is nationally offered, some states offer tax or other benefits for those who use their home state's plan, so it is a good idea to check with one's home state plan and to compare it with other plans. Unlike 529 college savings plans where more than one account can be opened for the same beneficiary, only one ABLE account can be opened for each eligible individual.

Like 529 college savings accounts, earnings in an ABLE account grow tax-deferred, and withdrawals are tax-free when used for qualified expenses. Qualified expenses include, but are not limited to, education, housing, transportation, employment training and support, assistive technology and personal support services, health, prevention and wellness support, financial management and administrative services, legal fees, expenses for oversight and monitoring, and other expenses which help improve health, independence and/or quality of life.

In general, individuals are eligible to invest in ABLE accounts if the onset of their disability began prior to age 26, they are receiving benefits under Supplemental Security Income (SSI) and/or Social Security Disability Insurance (SSDI), and/or if a licensed physician provides a written diagnosis of their condition. Please note that is possible that the age of onset will be adjusted upward in the future. Check with specific ABLE plans and/or with the two resources listed above for the most current information about ABLE plans and further details.

Additionally, individuals can invest in both 529 college savings and ABLE plans at the same time. Lastly, it should be noted that prior to December 31, 2025, up to $15,000 (or the current annual ABLE account contribution limit) can be rolled over from a 529 college savings plan to an ABLE account for the same beneficiary, or to an ABLE account of a family member of the 529 college savings account beneficiary.

Bank Savings Accounts. Traditional bank savings accounts are fully insured by the FDIC for up to $250,000 but as a trade-off to that safety, they typically earn very low interest. Also, unlike 529 college savings plans where earnings grow tax-deferred, interest on traditional bank accounts or certificates of deposit are taxed. With limited growth potential, saving exclusively in a traditional bank account for higher education expenses may make it harder to reach your financial goals. Additionally, since there is no restriction on use, you'll have an easier time accessing your funds for other purposes which could make it harder to stay on track with saving for college. Lastly, if you establish the bank account as a custodial account (see UGMA/UTMA section below), financial aid treatment will be less favorable than with a 529 college savings plan and you will lose control of the savings once your child turns 18 or 21, depending on state law.

Coverdell Education Savings Accounts. These accounts, previously called Education IRAs, grow tax-free and can be used for elementary and secondary school in addition to various forms of higher education. Unlike Roth IRAs (described below), the accounts do not require the contributor to have income, but there are maximum income limits for those who contribute. Like 529 college savings plans, contributions are made after-tax and are not deductible, grow tax-free, and when withdrawals are made to pay for qualified higher education expenses (as defined earlier), they are not subject to federal tax.

Additionally, they have the same asset protection as 529 college savings accounts, as described in Chapter 14, *Sites You Won't Want to Miss: Considering the Often-Overlooked Additional Benefits of Saving for College*. In contrast to 529 college savings plans, these accounts have significantly lower annual contribution limits (currently $2,000), account owners are subject to income limitations (currently, a contributor's modified adjusted gross income must be less than $110,000, or $220,000 for those filing a joint tax return). Also, unless the account beneficiary has special needs, the account assets must be used by age 30.

Roth IRAs. These are tax-deferred investment vehicles that are typically used as an investment for retirement, but they may also be used to fund qualified higher education expenses. Investors like the flexibility of being able to use these accounts for retirement if the money isn't fully needed for higher education. Unlike 529 college savings accounts, however, those who contribute to Roth IRAs must have earned income equal to or greater than the amount contributed annually.

In further contrast to 529 college savings accounts, the annual contribution limits are relatively low (currently $6,000, or $7,000 if account owner is 50 or over) and subject to phaseout based on account owner income which is required for account establishment and funding. Additionally, while the value of a Roth IRA is excluded from the Expected Family Contribution for federal financial aid analysis, a Roth withdrawal used to pay for higher education expenses can be considered untaxed income for the student or parent, and may be considered in future financial aid calculations along with the earnings portion of any withdrawal.

Uniform Gifts and Uniform Transfers to Minors Act Accounts (UGMA/UTMAs). These are typically taxable accounts that a custodian (often a parent or other adult in a child's life) controls until the child (beneficiary) reaches age 18 or 21 depending on state law, at which time ownership and control of funds transfers to the beneficiary. Parents typically set them up with financial services firms or banks and they can invest in a broad range of options including insured bank accounts or mutual funds. While the funds can be used for higher education, there is no requirement that they must be. They simply must be used for the benefit of the minor for whom the account was established. In contrast to 529 college savings plans, once the account beneficiary becomes an adult (otherwise referred to as reaching the age of termination), assets in these accounts are within their control and can be used for any purpose regardless of parent or account custodian preferences. Additionally, these accounts have a less favorable treatment when determining the Expected Family Contribution for federal financial aid purposes, as 20% of these assets are expected to be available to pay for higher education costs.

While you can set up 529 accounts as custodial accounts and can transfer proceeds from the sale of custodial account assets into 529 accounts, it is important that you fully understand the implications of doing so. See Chapter 15, *Taking the Scenic Route: Exploring*

Advanced Applications of 529 College Savings Plans for important information about setting 529 accounts up with UGMA/UTMA classification or when making UGMA/UTMA contributions into 529 plan accounts.

Mutual Fund or Other Taxable Investment Accounts. In contrast to 529 college savings accounts, these are taxable accounts that can be used for any purpose. Typically, interest, non-qualified dividends, and short-term capital gains are taxed to the owner at ordinary income rates while long-term capital gains and qualified dividends are taxed at long-term capital gains rates. Like 529 college savings accounts, the account owner retains control and for federal financial aid purposes, these accounts are considered parental assets if owned by a student's parent (up to 5.64% will be considered available to pay for higher education).

Annuities and/or Life Insurance. Many personal finance experts advise against using life insurance products to prepare for college costs. Some investors, however, are attracted to life insurance and annuity products because of their flexibility in use and because they generally do not count as assets for federal financial aid calculation purposes and have favorable tax features. When money is withdrawn, however, the value can count as untaxed income to the student and adversely affect financial aid eligibility in coming years. Additionally, in contrast to most 529 college savings plans, there are sometimes hefty initial and ongoing fees and commissions charged. Lastly, in the case of life insurance, withdrawing money reduces the death benefit value of the policy.

113

KEY TAKE-AWAYS

❑ You can utilize more than one type of 529 plan or other type of savings/investment vehicle at the same time. 529 prepaid tuition plans, for example, can complement 529 college savings plans. If you live in a state with a prepaid tuition plan or if you are interested in a prepaid plan for private colleges, be sure to learn more about these options.

❑ ABLE plans are a useful savings tool for persons with disabilities and can be used on their own or as a complement to 529 college savings plans.

❑ It's difficult to find a savings vehicle that has every single attribute you are seeking as there are pros and cons to each. Nonetheless, failing to save while looking for *the* perfect vehicle loses you valuable time. What's most important is that you start saving and continue saving.

❑ With the exception of ABLE plans and certain 529 prepaid plans, most of the alternative ways to save do not have a convenient and/or permissible way for others to easily and directly contribute. 529 college savings plans make it easy for friends, family, and employers to pitch in.

❑ Consider the advantages and disadvantages of the vehicles you decide to use.

CHAPTER 13
KEEPING YOUR EYES ON THE ROAD: RISKS & SPECIAL CONSIDERATIONS

While 529 college savings plans are viewed as the vehicle of choice by many to prepare for the cost of higher education, as with other investment types, there are benefits and trade-offs that you need to carefully consider prior to investing and over the life of your investment.

Accounts May Lose Value. As mentioned in the Disclosure section prior to Chapter 1, while these plans are called college *savings* plans, they are more accurately college *investing* plans and like all investments, they do involve some risk. The upside is that by investing in the financial markets, there is an opportunity for investment earnings that can be helpful in growing your assets to pay for the high cost of higher education. 529 college savings plans offer tax advantages as well. The downside is that you may lose money that you invested due to fluctuations in the financial markets and other factors.

Tax Consequences of Non-Qualified Withdrawals. Many investors appreciate the ability to earmark funds for higher education rather than co-mingling with savings for other purposes. Putting educational funds in a dedicated account is a benefit as it increases the chances that you will use the funds for education and not for other priorities. When, however, the funds in a 529 college savings plan are not used for covered expenses, there can be tax consequences. Withdrawals can be taken at any time from a 529 college savings account by the account owner, but those that do not fit within the definition of Qualified Withdrawals are considered *Non-Qualified Withdrawals*. Non-Qualified Withdrawals are subject to federal and state tax and a 10% federal penalty only on the earnings portion of the withdrawal (not on the portion of the withdrawal attributable to your contributions).

There is, however, special treatment for withdrawals that are taken based on the following circumstances:

1. Receipt of a Qualified Scholarship or Military Academy attendance

Should the beneficiary of the account receive a qualified scholarship or attend a Military Academy, the account owner may withdraw from the account up to the amount of the scholarship or in the case of the military academy attendance, the cost of education attributable to attendance. Such withdrawals may be paid to the account owner or beneficiary. Withdrawals made based on receipt of scholarships or attendance at military academies are not subject to the additional federal penalty tax. It is important to note that if the account owner selects a new beneficiary who is a family member of the beneficiary who received the scholarship, there will be no tax consequences at all.

2. Death of the Beneficiary

Should the beneficiary of the account die, the account owner may elect to withdraw all or a portion of the account for any use including payment to the estate of the beneficiary. Such a withdrawal would be considered non-qualified. While all non-qualified withdrawals are subject to applicable taxation on the earnings portion at the recipient's tax rate, withdrawals paid to the estate of the beneficiary are not subject to federal penalty tax on the earnings portion of the withdrawal. It is important to note that if the account owner selects a new beneficiary who is a member of the family of the deceased beneficiary, there will be no tax consequences at all.

3. Disability of the Beneficiary

Should the beneficiary of the account become disabled, the account owner may elect to withdraw all or a portion of the account for any use including payment to the disabled beneficiary. Such a withdrawal would be considered non-qualified. While all non-qualified withdrawals are subject to applicable taxation on the earnings portion at the recipient's tax rate, withdrawals made based on disability are not subject to the additional federal penalty. It is important to note that if the account owner selects a new beneficiary who is a member of the family of the disabled beneficiary, there will be no tax consequences at all.

Additionally, until December 31, 2025, unless extended, up to $15,000 (or the current annual ABLE account contribution limit) can be rolled over from a 529 college savings plan to an ABLE account for the same beneficiary, or to an ABLE account of a family member of the 529 college savings account beneficiary with no federal tax on contributions or earnings. Check with your 529 plan for specific details and for any state-specific considerations.

Program Costs. Fees and other expenses associated with your investment in a 529 college savings plan are an important consideration as they are paid out of the funds you invest in your account and thereby affect your account value. Your account's investment performance will be reduced by a variety of fees including program or investment management fees, expenses associated with the underlying investments in your account, and in some cases, an annual account maintenance fee. Since fees and expenses vary by 529 college savings plan, it's a good idea to compare one plan to another. Some plans which have annual account maintenance fees, for instance, waive them for clients who set up automatic contributions.

Fees and expenses are described in detail in 529 program offering materials and you should carefully review them. Fortunately, many 529 plans have reduced their fees over the years (and continue to do so), and there are many reasonably-priced options to choose from. Typically, as an investor you will pay annual fees related to the underlying investments in your portfolio(s). These expense ratios vary by the type and style of investments. For instance, index funds often have very low expenses while actively managed funds cost more.

To help you better understand fees and expenses, most 529 college savings plans will give an example on their website and/or in their program offering materials about the cost of a $10,000 investment in various investment options over various time periods. The ability to compare fees associated with a hypothetical $10,000 investment in one plan against that same investment in another plan can be helpful to you in seeing the impact of various programs' fees. Program fees should be among the many factors you consider when selecting a 529 plan. Since your account's performance will be net of fees, it is important to consider investment returns as well as fees, and to factor in the amount of time you will be invested in the account and subject to the fees. Keep in mind, however, that past performance is not a guarantee of future performance.

Beyond 529 plan fees, it's also important to note that accounts opened with the assistance of a financial professional may incur sales charges or additional ongoing expenses to compensate advisors for the services and support they provide you in connection with your 529 college savings plan. Some financial professionals may waive sales charges and may instead charge an hourly rate to advise you or an advisory fee based on your assets in the 529 plan or across all of your investments with the advisor. If you choose to use an advisor to help you with preparing for higher education expenses, you should be sure to determine exactly how they will be compensated as advice and guidance typically come at a cost. For more information on fees and expenses, visit your 529 program offering materials or speak with your advisor if you are working with one.

State Tax Considerations. While state tax credits or deductions can be valuable, it is important for you to understand exactly how they work. You should be sure to check the specific details of your state's tax treatment in connection with deductions or credits to determine any special conditions to which you may be subject. Keep in mind that state-based benefits should be one of many appropriately weighted factors to be considered when making an investment decision.

- **Who is eligible for deduction or credit.** In some states, only the account owner or the account owner's spouse may receive a deduction or credit for contributions made and in other states, any contributor who is a state taxpayer may take the deduction or credit. There are other variations as well. Further, in at least one state of which I am aware, a spouse may contribute to an account owned by the other spouse, but the contribution must be made from a banking account that is jointly owned by both spouses in order for the contribution to be eligible for the state tax deduction. Details like this are important to understand.

- **What plan is eligible for the deduction or credit.** Most states that have a state tax deduction or credit for contributions to 529 college savings plans make it available only for contributions to their own state's plan. There are a few states, however, that permit taxpayers to make contributions to their own state plan or any state plan and still take the deduction or credit. These are Arizona, Arkansas, Kansas, Minnesota, Missouri, Montana, and Pennsylvania.

- **Carry-forward.** In some states and in the District of Columbia, you may carry forward contributions to subsequent tax years if they exceed the amount that is allowed for a deduction or credit in a particular year. You'll want to utilize this benefit if it is available. Carry-forward treatment is currently available in Arkansas, Connecticut, Louisiana, Maryland, Ohio, Oklahoma, Oregon, Rhode Island, Virginia, Washington, D.C., West Virginia, and Wisconsin. Be sure to check the program offering materials for specific details.

• **What counts as a contribution.** In some states if you roll over funds from another state's 529 plan, the rollover will count as a contribution. In other states, it will not. In some states, only contributions made directly by the account owner or the account owner's spouse are eligible to be counted as contributions for tax credit or deduction purposes.

• **Recapture.** Some states may seek a tax recapture of deductions or credits previously taken if you roll over to an out-of-state plan or take a withdrawal that is considered non-qualified for state tax purposes. As noted in other sections, withdrawals for student loan repayment or K–12 expenses may be considered non-qualified by some states. Thus, these withdrawals may subject you to the recapture of contribution deductions or credits previously taken.

For these and all other state-specific details, check the 529 plan's offering materials.

Impact on Needs-Based Public Benefits. To qualify for most forms of government assistance such as food stamps (Supplemental

Nutrition Assistance Program, otherwise referred to as SNAP), medical assistance (Medicaid), cash assistance (TANF and SSI), and affordable housing (HUD), families must demonstrate that their income and assets are below a certain threshold. While the rules about whether 529 plan holdings are viewed as a countable resource are clear for certain forms of assistance in certain states or cities, there is not complete clarity across the United States. Therefore, you should check carefully to determine whether the value of your 529 college savings account could be viewed as a countable resource in determining your financial eligibility for needs-based benefits and whether disbursements from your account could affect your or your child's eligibility going forward. You should consult an advisor who is familiar with the state and federal benefits in which you participate or may seek to participate in the future, or contact the agencies that administer the benefits.

Limited Investment Change. While you can change your investment allocations for future contributions at any time prior to making them, you have limited opportunity to change the investment allocations for 529 college savings account contributions previously made (and any earnings thereon). Such changes are limited to twice per calendar year. You may, however, change your investment allocations on previous contributions and earnings whenever you change your account beneficiary to a family member of the current beneficiary.

Financial Aid. In addition to the minimal impact 529 college savings plans can have on federal financial aid eligibility as reviewed earlier in Chapter 4, you should consider the impact your 529 college savings account may have on state financial aid and institutional aid. You should also consider that in addition to requiring the FAFSA, some institutions (over 240 private colleges and universities) require the CSS Profile Form, which takes a more comprehensive look at a family's financial situation. The CSS Profile counts 529 plans for which the student is the beneficiary on the account, regardless of who owns the account. Lastly, you should consider the impact that 529 college savings plans owned by persons other than the custodial parent can have upon disbursement of those funds. While it is generally agreed that it is better to save than to rely on financial aid, you should consider any potential impact on eligibility.

Grandparent Considerations. Grandparents often play a very valuable role in funding college savings accounts for their grandchildren. They do not need to be the owner of a 529 account to contribute. In fact, in many cases they contribute to accounts owned by their adult children for which their grandchildren are the account beneficiaries. It's important to note that any third party (including grandparents and others) who contributes to an account they do not own forfeits any rights to their contributions once they've been made. The gift giver cannot, for instance, direct how the contribution is invested or when it is withdrawn and cannot obtain information about the account unless the account owner grants permission. Complete control of the account rests with the account owner (which is often a child's parent).

While many grandparents are comfortable contributing to an account established and owned by their adult child or someone else, some grandparents choose to open their own 529 college savings accounts for their grandchildren. When grandparents open accounts in their own names for the benefit of a grandchild, however, in addition to many benefits, there are also special issues that can arise that are worthy of consideration. These relate to both a grandparent's potential reliance on Medicaid and the potential financial impact of withdrawals from a grandparent's 529 college savings account on a grandchild's financial aid eligibility.

Grandparents and Medicaid. For elderly grandparents or those in poor health who are 529 college savings plan account owners and who may have the need to rely on Medicaid, there are special considerations. You may recall from Chapter 3 that account owners retain control of 529 accounts. Thus, for grandparents who may need to apply for Medicaid, the value of a 529 college savings account they own is considered a countable asset and may need to be spent down before Medicaid would begin providing nursing home or other assistance a grandparent may need. Even if a grandparent were to transfer the account to another, the timing of the transfer may still cause it to be counted as an asset owned by the grandparent.

Grandparents and Financial Aid Treatment. Because they are not owned by the student or the student's parents, funds in a

124

grandparent-owned 529 college savings account are not reportable on the Free Application for Federal Student Aid (FAFSA) that students and their parents file each year. As discussed previously, most colleges use the FAFSA to determine how much a family can afford to contribute toward college (Expected Family Contribution or EFC) and how much a student should be offered in terms of grants, scholarships and/or loans. The smaller the EFC, the greater the potential financial aid.

While there is no impact on financial aid while the assets are in a grandparent-owned account (since such account is not owned by the parents whose assets are the subject of the FAFSA application and thus, not reportable on the FAFSA), there are potentially adverse consequences once withdrawals are made to pay for a grandchild's higher education expenses. Such withdrawals are reported as unearned income on a grandchild's FAFSA form covering the period in which the withdrawal was made. The amount of the withdrawal can reduce the grandchild's financial aid eligibility by up to 50%. It is important to note that when filling out the FAFSA, you are using income and tax information from two years before the time you are applying. For example, if you complete the FAFSA in January 2021, you will be required to report your income and assets from 2019.

There are strategies for handling accounts owned by grandparents and other third parties that may help to avoid adverse financial aid consequences. For instance, distributions from grandparent accounts can be delayed until the student's third or fourth year of college (if the student is pursuing a four-year degree and has no plans to immediately pursue graduate school) since the lookback period for the FAFSA is two years. If a grandparent withdraws funds after January 1 of a four-year student's sophomore year or later after the FAFSA is filed, the withdrawal wouldn't have an impact if the student is graduating in four years. The thought is that the student, if not pursuing graduate school immediately after, will be out of school by the time the withdrawal consequences would surface for financial aid application purposes as they would not be filing a FAFSA to qualify for yet another year of financial aid.

Also, subject to state tax considerations and plan rules, grandparents may change ownership of their 529 college savings account by transferring the entire balance to the child's parent. Another approach for grandparents is to consider waiting until the grandchild receives a financial aid award letter and changing ownership of only a portion of the grandparent-owned account (the amount that is needed for the following school year) by transferring that amount to the parent-owned 529 account. Whether transferring all or a portion of the grandparent-owned account to the parent-owned account, a payment can then be made to the school from the parent-owned account. That way, the funds will not show up as untaxed income to the student because the withdrawal is from a parent-owned account.

Check with a tax advisor about any tax implications resulting from change in ownership and check with an individual who is knowledgeable about financial aid to ensure any approach you pursue will be the most advantageous for your student.

Non-Custodial Parents and Other Relatives as Account Owners. The same concerns that apply to grandparents and financial aid can also apply to non-custodial parents and others. Understanding the implications of accounts owned by persons other than custodial parents is critical. To the extent possible, it is also important that all parties including parents, students, grandparents, and/or other relatives who want to contribute to your child's education communicate with each other so that everyone can have the most favorable impact on your child without inadvertently causing financial aid concerns. It is important to note, however, that institutions requiring the CSS Profile Form in addition to the FAFSA count all 529 accounts for which the student is the account beneficiary, regardless of who owns them.

Divorce. Divorcing parents should consider that while contributions are treated as a completed gift to the beneficiary of the account, the assets in a 529 college savings account remain under the control of the account holder. As such, the account owner may change the account beneficiary, transfer funds from an account of one beneficiary to the account of another beneficiary, or withdraw the funds for a non-qualified use, subject to tax and penalty. Also, as mentioned above, distributions from 529 college savings accounts owned by someone other than a custodial parent could have an impact on a student's financial aid in subsequent years following a distribution. Parents should seek advice and guidance of legal counsel about the treatment of 529 college savings accounts in connection with a marital separation or divorce.

Death. Naming a successor account owner on your 529 account assures that the account can be transferred smoothly and automatically to the successor upon your death without going through probate. The successor account owner who you name will assume all the rights of you as the original owner. This includes the right to change the account beneficiary and request withdrawals for any purpose. You must have confidence that your named successor will fulfill your original wishes for the account. Since 529 college savings plan accounts can be owned by trusts, it is possible to name a trust as a successor instead of an individual. The terms of the trust can ensure that the assets are used in the manner you intended. You should consult an attorney or other professional about including 529 assets in your will and about the possibility of naming a trust as successor on your 529 account.

Change in Beneficiary. A change of beneficiary or transfer to an account of another beneficiary may result in federal gift tax or generation-skipping tax consequences if the new beneficiary is two or more generations younger than the replaced beneficiary or not a "member of the family" of the replaced beneficiary. You should consult a tax or legal advisor before making a change in beneficiaries.

Using 529 Accounts for K–12. If you intend to take withdrawals of up to $10,000 annually from your 529 college savings account for certain K–12 expenses (as described in Chapter 15), you should make sure that the investments you select either on your own or with the help of a financial advisor align with the timeframe for use. Many 529 college savings plan investment options are designed with the assumption that they will be used when a child reaches college age. If your intention is to use some or all of the funds sooner, you will want to make sure you choose an investment option that is appropriate for a shorter investment horizon.

Also, while withdrawals for certain K–12 expenses may be made without federal tax implications, you should check to see whether such withdrawals are considered qualified from a state tax perspective and if not, whether there are adverse tax implications. In some states, for instance, when a distribution is used for K–12 tuition, a taxpayer who previously received a state tax credit or state tax deduction for a contribution may need to repay a portion of the credit or deduction previously taken.

Using 529 Accounts to Repay Student Loan Debt. While such withdrawals may be made without federal tax implications (as described in Chapter 3), you should check to see whether such withdrawals are considered qualified from a state tax perspective and if not, whether there are adverse tax implications.

UGMA/UTMA Implications. If you are a custodian of a UGMA/UTMA account, you may be able to open a 529 account for the same beneficiary and transfer proceeds from the sale of assets previously held in the UGMA/UTMA account into a 529 account, subject to the laws of the state where you opened the UGMA/UTMA account. As custodian, you will serve as the Account Owner and the 529 account will be titled in such a way to reflect that it contains UGMA/UTMA assets.

There are important considerations, however, that you should be aware of when transferring UGMA/UTMA funds or when setting up a 529 account with an UGMA/UTMA classification:

• Unlike a 529 account that does not contain assets of a custodial nature in which the account owner maintains full control, assets in an UGMA/UTMA classified 529 college savings account can ONLY be used for the benefit of the beneficiary and cannot be withdrawn by the account owner for any other purpose.

• Additionally, the beneficiary on the account cannot be changed to another future student. In fact, when the beneficiary reaches the age of termination (age 18 or 21, depending on the state in which the custodial account was established) and the custodianship terminates, the account beneficiary is legally entitled to take control of the account and may become the account owner.

Since the classification of UGMA/UTMA in a 529 account takes on certain characteristics that make it more limited than a non-custodial 529 account that does not contain such funds, it is advisable to refrain from combining UGMA/UTMA contributions with other assets— because all future deposits into an UGMA/UTMA 529 account will acquire the same characteristics once deposited. Assets cannot be withdrawn for other purposes, cannot be transferred to a family member of the original beneficiary, and become the beneficiary's upon reaching the age of termination. Instead, you may want to set up a separate non-custodial 529 account into which you can make additional contributions to avoid the limitations caused by the custodial classification.

Be sure to consult with a financial professional if you are working with one or with the 529 plan with which you are investing directly for specific details on this topic.

KEY TAKE-AWAYS

❑   Read the program materials carefully and pose questions if you have them to the 529 plan's call center or to an advisor if you are working with one.

❑   Talk to anyone, including grandparents, who may open a college savings account for your child, so that you can coordinate the effort.

❑   Pay careful attention to the implications of funding a 529 college savings account with UGMA/UTMA contributions.

❑   Make certain you understand the cost of investing in the plan you select.

CHAPTER 14

SITES YOU WON'T WANT TO MISS: CONSIDERING THE OFTEN-OVERLOOKED ADDITIONAL BENEFITS OF SAVING FOR COLLEGE

Besides the most obvious benefits of saving in advance for higher education goals, there are valuable additional benefits that are frequently overlooked. These additional benefits can have a positive impact on both you and your student.

Increasing College-Going Expectations and Aspirations. The establishment of an account earmarked for college can help to create an expectation that higher education will be a part of the future of the child for whom the account is established. With this in mind, it's important to let your child(ren) know you or others are saving for them and believe in their potential. The existence of college savings accounts can help young people view higher education as an achievable goal.

Research suggests that even a small amount of college savings can increase college attendance and completion.[10] A low- and moderate-income child with educational savings of $499 or less prior to

---

[10] Elliott, W. III, Song, H-a, and Nam, I. "Small-Dollar Children's Savings Accounts and Children's College Outcomes by Income Level." *Children & Youth Services Review*, March 2013, 35(3), pp. 560-571. https://doi.org/10.1016/j.childyouth.2012.12.003

reaching college age is approximately three times more likely to enroll in college and four times more likely to graduate than a child with no savings account. Further, saving in a 529 plan is a healthy financial behavior that can be observed by the children for whom you are investing and it opens the door to various topics that can be explored and discussed as a family depending on the children's ages.

Discussing Values, Interests, and Priorities. Letting your child know you are saving for their educational future presents a great opportunity to explain the value you place on higher learning and why. This also presents an opportunity to discuss the importance of establishing priorities and distinguishing between needs and wants to help achieve financial goals. Making your child(ren) aware that you are making tradeoffs as a family in order for them go to college and have a rewarding career when they grow up will help put into context some of the decisions you are making. It will also help them understand just how committed you are to their future and what a big but manageable undertaking it is to prepare for long-term goals. Lastly, it will help them to understand that what we do today impacts tomorrow.

Exploring Academic and Career Interests. Depending on the age of your child, saving for college also lends itself to conversations about your child's interests and aspirations and the forms of education that may help with the contributions your child wants to make to the world from a career and/or values perspective. Former Google Education Evangelist Jaime Casup (an advisor for the firm with which I am employed) recommends that instead of asking children what they want to be when they grow up, ask them what problem(s) they want to solve in the world. This will help you to identify some of the issues that your child deeply cares about so that together you can consider what it may take in terms of education and experiences to get them into a position in which they can make an impact.

Modeling Healthy Financial Behavior. As with many forms of education, the seeds of financial literacy are first planted and nourished at home. Parents often serve not only as Chief Operating Officers but also as Chief Education and Chief Financial Officers of their families. Whether a single parent or sharing the responsibility of parenting with another, the examples we set as financial role models can have a lasting impact on our children. Your children will learn more from you by what they see you do than by what you say. Investing in their future a little at a time is a great way to lead by example as a parent.

Here are a number of topics you can consider discussing in connection with saving for college:

- **Designating savings.** Exploring the differences between short- and long-term goals can help children recognize the importance of earmarking funds for different purposes versus putting them in one account or one piggy bank or jar. Through this conversation, you might explain why having an emergency (or "rainy day") fund for your family can be extremely helpful. You can also explain why you chose to specifically designate funds for higher education in a college savings plan versus a more general use saving or investing account that includes savings for a broader range of goals. As children receive money from allowance or gifts, you can help them to decide how to allocate those funds. They may want to divide them into categories such as what they will spend, save for short or long-term goals, and/or give away.

- **Creating a plan.** Explaining that long-term goals start with both visualizing and quantifying what you want to achieve is important, as is the topic of working backwards from the future goal to determine exactly what steps need to be taken to get you there. This is a great way to show the value of having a plan and to demonstrate that small, consistent steps over time can help achieve big goals.

- **Reviewing expenditures.** As mentioned in Chapter 9, *Creating a Travel Budget: Saving More by Spending Less and Incorporating Minimalism*, what you spend has a lot to do with how much you will be able to save. In an age-appropriate way, reviewing elements of your family's budget can help children understand that eliminating unnecessary expenditures can help with savings goals. This enables you to show that it's not only what you *earn* but also what you *spend* that has a lot to do with what you'll be able to save.

- **Incorporating other topics.** As children grow in age and understanding, 529 account(s) can be a basis for a discussion about how the money you set aside can grow thanks to *compounding*. Additionally, taking time to review the particular investments you selected and how they've performed over time can lend itself to a discussion of *risk and reward*. And of course, if you are so inclined, you could also discuss *taxable* versus *tax-free* investing.

Being a positive financial role model and providing financial know-how to your children are among the greatest and longest-lasting gifts you can give. The more they can learn about the value, investment, and management of money, the better position they'll be in as they grow into independent and responsible adults. The seeds you plant today can help to develop strong roots and can have a priceless impact on those you love.

Accessing State-Specific Benefits. In addition to state tax deductions or credits for 529 college savings account contributions (as discussed in Chapter 3 and in the Appendix), there are other valuable benefits that are available in certain states. These include:

- **Matching Grants/Seed Money.** Some states (or communities) offer seed money to get you started, matching grants (to match some of what you've contributed), and/or other incentives to provide support and encouragement to 529 plan investors.

- **Child Development (or Children's Savings) Accounts.** Several states have passed legislation to automatically open and make a deposit into a 529 account for all state-resident newborns.[11] Additionally, some cities, community organizations, non-profits, and

---

[11] Clancy, Margaret M., Sherraden, Michael, and Beverly, Sondra G. "Child Development Accounts at Scale: Sample State Legislation," *CSD Policy Summary*, No. 19-46, November 2019. Center for Social Development, Washington University, St. Louis, MO. https://doi.org/10.7936/cptg-2n77

private entities have developed programs to make deposits for cohorts of students. Known as Child Development Accounts (CDAs), or sometimes referred to as Children's Savings Accounts (CSAs), the goal is to improve early developmental outcomes and eventually increase postsecondary success, especially for children in financially vulnerable households.

• **State Financial Aid and Asset Protection.** Some states offer favorable treatment in determining state financial aid and special asset protection treatment for 529 college savings accounts. Be sure to check your state or community to see if any of the benefits mentioned above may be available to you.

Obtaining Creditor Protection. Subject to certain conditions and limitations, some assets that have been contributed to a 529 plan account are protected in federal bankruptcy proceedings. To be protected, the 529 account beneficiary must be a child, stepchild, grandchild, or step-grandchild of the individual who files for bankruptcy protection. In addition, subject to the following limits, contributions made to all 529 plan accounts for the same beneficiary are protected as follows:

• Contributions made less than 365 days before the bankruptcy filing are <u>not</u> protected.

• Contributions made between 365 and 720 days before the bankruptcy filing are protected up to $6,225 (as adjusted for inflation).

- Contributions made more than 720 days before the bankruptcy filing are fully protected.

It's important to note that under state law, protections vary.

Stories from the Road

A former client of mine told me that she always makes sure to ask the future students in her life "*Where* will you be going to college?" versus "*Will* you be going to college?" This reminds them of the expectation that they will be attending college and reinforces her belief in them and their future.

A Peek into My Journey

When I think back to where and how I gathered my earliest insights into financial matters, I vividly recall a number of scenarios, variations of which were repeated many times throughout my early years. These include seeing my mom concentrate into the late hours of the night on her budget and bill paying, accompanying her and my three siblings to our local bank with coins we had diligently saved and proudly having our deposits reflected in our passbooks, and relying on our rainy day fund when our car broke down or other unexpected expenses arose. While we had very little money to spare, it always felt comforting to know that my mom was paying careful attention to our family's finances and that we had some savings safely tucked away to rely on.

In addition to incorporating many of the financial lessons my mom taught me as a child, I also used our 529 plan accounts and the topic of saving for college to drive some of those lessons home for my son in an easy-to-understand way. Twice annually, we took our son to cash in the coins he diligently saved and this enabled us to deposit a total of $600 a year on average into his college savings account.

We also shared with our son that we were taking a certain amount out of our paychecks for his college savings account to help reach our goal so that he could avoid having the level of student loan debt that we both had to repay with interest after obtaining our degrees. Telling him about our financial situations as students and the stress that student loan repayment placed on us helped put into context why we were so focused on saving for him.

KEY TAKE-AWAYS

❏ Explore and make use of the additional benefits of saving with 529 college savings plans that go well beyond the obvious ones.

❏ Use your account as an opportunity to remind your children that you believe in them and in their educational and career aspirations.

❏ Use your 529 college savings account as a vehicle to educate your children about the importance of planning ahead for long-term goals.

CHAPTER 15

TAKING THE SCENIC ROUTE: EXPLORING ADVANCED APPLICATIONS OF 529 COLLEGE SAVINGS PLANS

There are various ways 529 plans can be utilized that are valuable for you to know about.

K–12 Expenses. 529 plan account owners may make withdrawals to pay for tuition expenses in connection with enrollment or attendance at an elementary or secondary public, private, or religious school (K–12 tuition expenses) up to $10,000 per year in the aggregate per beneficiary.

529 college savings plan account owners are authorized to withdraw up to $10,000 per year per beneficiary for K–12 tuition expenses without paying federal taxes on account earnings or a federal penalty. State tax treatment, however, needs to be checked carefully to see if such withdrawals are considered qualified from a state tax perspective and if not, whether there are adverse state tax consequences.

Student Loan Repayment. 529 account owners may make withdrawals to pay the principal or interest on any qualified education loan (as defined in Internal Revenue Code Section 221(d)) of the beneficiary or a sibling of the beneficiary but not to exceed $10,000 per individual. State tax treatment, however, needs to be checked carefully to see if such withdrawals are considered qualified from a state tax perspective and if not, whether there are adverse state tax consequences.

Apprenticeships. The federal definition of Qualified Higher Education Expenses includes expenses for fees, books, supplies, and equipment required for participation in an apprenticeship program registered and certified with the Secretary of Labor under section 1 of the National Apprenticeship Act (29 U.S.C. 50).

Account Ownership by Entities and Trusts. As mentioned in Chapter 3, 529 college savings plan accounts may be established by state or local governments, or tax-exempt organizations described in section 501(c)(3) of the Internal Revenue Code. They may also be established by most types of legal entities, including trusts, provided their purposes and powers permit.

529 college savings plan accounts are viewed as easier to administer than trust accounts for non-profits and other entities with scholarship or children's savings account (CSA) programs, also referred to as children's development account (CDA) programs. Non-profits and other entities can use these accounts to invest scholarship funds for future students.

Scholarship Accounts. A state or local government, or agency, instrumentality, or tax-exempt organization may establish an account as part of a scholarship program operated by such government or organization. Governments and tax-exempt organizations select the account's investment options on their own or with the help of a financial professional.

While a 529 college savings plan is not a tax-saving investment for 501(c)(3) organizations because these organizations are not subject to tax, these accounts are often preferred by charitable organizations over other types of accounts for a number of reasons.

First, unlike traditional 529 college savings accounts owned by individuals, 501(c)(3) organizations need not name a beneficiary at the time of account opening. Instead, beneficiaries are named at a future time when the recipients of scholarships are chosen just before distributions are made on behalf of the beneficiaries.

Second, unlike 529 college savings accounts owned by individuals, the 529 account owned by a 501(c)(3) is not subject to the 529 college savings plan's maximum contribution or balance limit over the life of the account. This provides the organization with tremendous flexibility in building scholarship programs.

Third, low management fees and professional investment management services are appealing to charitable organizations.

Lastly, the recordkeeping provided by 529 college savings plans reduces the administrative burden on the charitable organization that owns the scholarship account.

For these and other reasons, 529 college savings accounts are often the preferred vehicles for many Children's Savings Account (CSA) or Child Development Account (CDA) programs as well. These programs, as briefly discussed in Chapter 14, help to improve college-going expectations in the participating children and their families. The most rigorous research on CDAs comes from an on-going experiment across the state of Oklahoma. Researchers at the Center for Social Development at Washington University in St. Louis have published numerous peer-reviewed studies showing that the CDA has positive financial and non-financial impacts for both parents and children.[12] These effects include more positive outlook by parents, better parenting, higher educational expectations, and improved child development. Effects are sometimes strongest for the most disadvantaged families.[13]

529 college savings accounts are often preferred vehicles for these purposes (over other options like bank accounts) because contributions are invested in the financial markets with the support of professional investment managers and as such, have an opportunity for growth that goes beyond modest interest rates associated with traditional bank accounts. "In short, no existing

[12] Clancy, Margaret M., Sherraden, Michael, and Beverly, Sondra G. "SEED for Oklahoma Kids Wave 3: Extending Rigorous Research and a Successful Policy Model," *CSD Research Brief*, No. 19–06, March 2019. Center for Social Development, Washington University, St. Louis, MO. https://doi.org/10.7936/zx2j-0543

[13] Huang, J., Beverly, S.G., Kim, Clancy, M.M., and Sherraden, M. "Financially Vulnerable Families Reap Multiple Benefits from Child Development Accounts," *CSD Research Brief*, No. 19–40, October 2019. Center for Social Development, Washington University, St. Louis, MO. https://doi.org/10.7936/akd8-d690

financial platform other than 529 plans provides a comparable combination of features required for CDAs."[14]

Employer Involvement. Employers are uniquely positioned to pass along valuable education to their employee base about the existence and usefulness of 529 college savings plans. Doing so helps employees plan for higher education costs and avoid or minimize student loan debt in the future. With nearly 65% of Americans unfamiliar with these plans according to the Gift of College May 2020 "Paying for College" Survey, providing education about 529 college savings plans can be a priceless benefit. At little or no cost coupled with minimal involvement by the employer, 529 plan administrators or third-party services providers can facilitate both employee education and payroll deduction to 529 college savings plans. Some have the ability to facilitate an employer matching contribution as well. As a voluntary financial wellness benefit, 529 college savings plans (and ABLE plans, as discussed in Chapter 12) can be life changing. By offering 529 plans as a benefit, employers can empower employees to experience less stress and have brighter financial outcomes.

For national employers who may find it complicated to offer just one 529 college savings plan because of employees residing in multiple states, there are platforms such as the one I work with, Gift of College

---

[14] Sherraden, M., Clancy, M., and Beverly, S. "Taking Child Development Accounts to Scale: Ten Key Policy Design Elements," *CSD Policy Brief*, No. 18-08, February 2018. Center for Social Development, Washington University, St. Louis, MO. https://csd.wustl.edu/18-08/

At-Work, that are plan-neutral and can facilitate contributions to most any 529 college savings plan (and ABLE plan) so that an employer's benefits team doesn't need to pick one plan over another. Introducing 529 plans as an employee benefit can help with employee recruitment, retention, and engagement. Employers also have the ability to match employee contributions or make one-off contributions to lend a hand. Lightening the load of employees can go a long way in improving and maintaining job satisfaction.

Given the positive impact that 529 college savings plans can have on employees and their families, employers of all sizes across the United States should consider offering 529 college savings plans as a voluntary employee benefit. According to the Society for Human Resource Management's 2019 Employee Benefits survey only 11% of employers are currently doing so.

Momentum is building as employers are recognizing the value of joining a movement to help their employees' families avoid student loan debt by planning ahead for higher education costs. While there is currently no federal tax incentive for employers to offer 529 plans as an employee benefit, I am hopeful that someday there will be. A number of states do offer state tax benefits for employers to contribute to employee 529 college savings plans. These currently include Arkansas, Colorado, Illinois (for taxable years ending on or before 12/31/2021 unless extended), Idaho, Nebraska (beginning 1/1/2021), Nevada, Utah, and Wisconsin.

As I stated earlier, I am so grateful to have learned about 529 college savings plans through my employment before my son was even born and to now have been able to put him through college by investing in them with the help of my employer.

Employees: Ask your employer about offering access to 529 college savings and/or ABLE plans as an employee benefit.

Employers: Consider this priceless benefit for your employees. Whether or not you are able to offer an employer financial contribution or match as an added incentive, the education you will provide can positively impact the lives of your employees and their families. You'll have a chance to take a bite out of student loan debt by helping your employees and their children avoid it by introducing them to 529 college savings plans. Additionally, for those employees whose families are impacted by disability-related expenses, you'll be offering a path to improved financial security by introducing them to ABLE plans.

Investing in Multiple 529 Plans. You may open multiple 529 college savings accounts for the same beneficiary and there are a variety of reasons you may want to do so. This approach is often pursued by those who may want to limit their annual contributions to their state plan to take advantage of any available state tax deduction or credit that is limited to investments in one's home state 529 college savings plan—while also investing in a second, preferred out-of-state plan. Others may wish to participate in a specific matching grant or seed money program associated with their home state 529 college savings plan but who also wish to invest in other plans at the suggestion of their financial advisor or for diversification. For instance, you may want to invest in your home state's program in order to avail yourself of an annual state tax deduction, but you would also like to invest in an option that your home state's program does not have (such as one that is FDIC insured). Regardless of the approach you pursue, keep in mind that the total you invest in one or more plans should align with your reasonable expectations for the cost of your beneficiary's education after high school.

Creating an Education Legacy for Future Generations.

Contributing to a 529 college savings plan is a great way to leave an education legacy for generations to come. Because there is generally no time limit on how long money can remain invested in a 529 account, contributions can be used for the current named beneficiary and then changed to other members of that beneficiary's family in the future. See Chapter 4 for definition of family member. If the child for whom you set up the account doesn't need or use the account's value, it can be saved and eventually switched to that child's child.

Wealth Transfer. Contributing to a 529 college savings plan also can be extremely helpful to individuals (typically grandparents) who wish to reduce the size of their taxable estates.

Annual Gift Tax Exclusion and Completed Gifts. There's no federal gift tax on contributions up to $15,000 per beneficiary per year as these contributions qualify for the annual gift tax exclusion (currently $15,000 for individuals, $30,000 for spouses who split gifts; periodically adjusted for inflation). As mentioned in the section above about control, contributions to 529 college savings plans are considered completed gifts to the beneficiary and are removed from the donor's estate. Stated otherwise, for federal gift, estate, and generation-skipping transfer tax purposes, contributions to a 529 college savings account are not subject to tax as long as they do not exceed the annual federal gift tax exclusion.

Five-Year Gift Averaging (also referred to as Five-Year Forward or Accelerated Gifting). A special provision in Section 529 of the Internal Revenue Code allows you to accelerate your gift giving by contributing up to five years' worth of annual exclusion gifts per beneficiary in a single year. At the time of publication of this book, the annual exclusion is $15,000, however, it is periodically adjusted for inflation. If you (or another donor such as a grandparent) are a single filer, you can currently contribute up to $75,000 per beneficiary in any one year and if you, or another donor, are part of a married couple which files jointly, you and your spouse can currently contribute up to $150,000.

Five-Year Gift Averaging is not just for the wealthy. If you are able to contribute more than the annual gift allowance, you can use this feature and report your gift on IRS Form 709.

It's important to note that no additional gifts can be made to the same beneficiary during these five years if such gifts would cause you or your spouse to exceed these maximums. Any excess gift would trigger gift tax and would be applied against the donor's lifetime gift tax exemption. Should the donor die during the five-year period, 20% of the contribution must be included in their taxable estate for each missed year. Stated otherwise, the donor must live one day into the fifth year to avoid a pro rata portion of the gift being added back to the donor's estate for estate tax purposes. IRS Form 709 (Gift Tax Return) should be filed in any year when a five-year gift is made to a 529 college savings account.

Grandparents and Required Minimum Distributions. If they do not need the distributions to meet expenses, grandparents might choose to fund a 529 plan with required minimum distributions from an IRA. In a 529 account, any earnings on those reinvested assets would grow tax-deferred whereas earnings would be taxed should they be deposited in another type of account like a bank or brokerage account.

Transferring a Trust (UGMA or UTMA) Account to a 529 Account. As discussed in Chapter 13, *Keeping Your Eyes on the Road: Risks & Special Considerations*, it is important to pay careful attention when contributing proceeds from a sale of assets held in a custodial account to a 529 college savings account. Since the classification of UGMA/UTMA in a 529 account takes on certain characteristics that make it more limited than a non-custodial 529 account that does not contain such funds, it is advisable to refrain from combining UGMA/UTMA funds with other assets as all future deposits into an UGMA/UTMA 529 account will acquire the same characteristics once deposited. Assets cannot be withdrawn for other purposes, cannot be transferred to a family member of the original beneficiary, and become the beneficiary's upon reaching the age of majority. Instead, you may want to set up a separate non-custodial 529 account into which you can make additional contributions to avoid the limitations caused by the trust classification.

Purchase of Real Estate. Parents of children attending college away from home sometimes consider purchasing a home or condo in the parent's name near the location of their child's college and charge their child (and any roommates who live with their child) rent as they attend college. Since off-campus living expenses are considered qualified expenses under 529 college savings plans provided students are attending an eligible school at least half time and expenses do not exceed the college's room and board costs as published in the cost of attendance (or the actual expense), parents wonder whether they can take tax-free withdrawals from their 529 plan to cover their child's portion of the monthly rent. You should seek advice from a tax advisor if you are considering a strategy such as this as there is a lot to consider. For instance, if you decide to charge your child rent in order to pay your child's housing expense with funds from a 529 plan, your taxable income and tax liability will be increased by that rent and any rent received from your child's roommates.

In addition to other issues to consider, you'll want to weigh the increased income and taxes against any eligible tax deductions you may be able to take in connection with owning a piece of investment real estate.

KEY TAKE-AWAYS

❑ Grandparents can benefit from a number of 529 plan features.

❑ Accelerated gifting can be helpful to anyone who wishes to contribute more than the annual gift exclusion in a year.

❑ When considering a withdrawal of funds for K–12 tuition or for student loan repayment, be sure to review your state tax treatment as there may be an adverse impact.

❑ In addition to individual account owners, entities, trusts, and non-profits can be 529 college savings plan account owners and can set up scholarship accounts.

❑ Employers can play an important role in helping employees avoid student loan debt by educating them about 529 college savings plans and providing them with a convenient way to contribute.

CHAPTER 16

ROUGH ROAD AHEAD:
EXAMINING THE COST OF MISSING THE
ON-RAMP AND NOT PLANNING AHEAD

As parents, we clearly want the very best for our children. Even before they arrive, we spend a tremendous amount of time researching the best car seat and making sure we install it correctly, child-proofing our homes, and acquiring many other items to keep our children healthy and safe. Their well-being is our top concern. There are many lists of must-have items that new parents refer to but what typically isn't included—but really should be—is a 529 college savings account.

When it comes to something as important as preparing for the cost of higher education, as parents, we often allow life to get in the way and put college savings on the back burner for years after their child arrives. With the best of intentions, many intend to begin saving "someday" but in many cases, that day never comes.

Not planning ahead for the cost of something as critical and costly as higher education creates several very heavy loads to bear. When it comes time for child(ren) to graduate from high school and pursue higher learning, many parents wind up carrying a tremendous weight of regret for having not planned ahead for college or career training— or deep regret for having not started saving sooner.

NEW BABY
MUST HAVE LIST

- ☐ Crib & Mattress
- ☐ Infant Car Seat
- ☐ Crib Sheets & Bumper
- ☐ Infant Tub
- ☐ Changing Table
- ☐ Stroller
- ☐ First Aid Kit
- ☐ Diaper Bag with Changing Pad

- ☐ Nursing Supplies
- ☐ Front-facing Baby Carrier
- ☐ Bottles
- ☐ Diapers, Wipes & Creams
- ☐ Baby Monitor
- ☐ Onesies
- ☐ Receiving Blankets

☐ 529 College Savings Account

"The days are long, but the years are short."[15]

~Gretchen Rubin, *The Happiness Project*

In these scenarios, the child winds up with a high level of educational debt and faces an uphill challenge in paying it back over many years following graduation. Or alternatively, the child winds up not pursuing higher education at all or drops out due to financial stress with student loans to repay but with no degree to show for the debt.

[15] Rubin, Gretchen. "The Years Are Short," *A Little Happier.* May 9, 2016, https://gretchenrubin.com/podcast-episode/daysarelong/

Another possibility is that the parents wind up borrowing from their retirement accounts or taking out parent loans on behalf of their children at a time when their focus should more appropriately be on preparing for retirement years and/or on caring for their own aging parents.

The choice is a clear one. You can save and invest now or borrow and repay tomorrow. When you save, you are earning interest and when you borrow, you are repaying interest.

As an example, if a parent invests $150/month ($5/day) over 18 years and receives a 5% return, over $52,000 can be accumulated to pay toward higher education expenses. If a parent does not save and instead has to borrow (or the child has to borrow) that same amount ($52,000) and pay it back over 10 years at a 3% interest rate, monthly payments would be $506/month and the total repaid would be over $60,000. Save $150 a month or repay over $500 a month. Saving helps you avoid the stress of repayment and thousands of dollars in interest payments.

Saving in advance helps you avoid both debt and regret.

SAVE OR REPAY?

SAVE
$150/Month
OR
REPAY
$506/Month

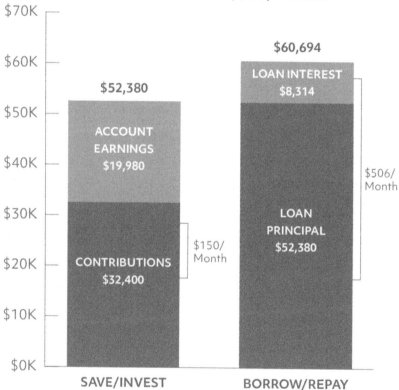

Assumptions: An investment of $150/month over 18 years with a 5% rate of return compounded monthly results in $52,380 in savings. Borrowing the same amount of $52,380 and repaying it over 10 years at a 3% interest rate = $60,694 or a student loan payment of $506/month.

KEY TAKE-AWAYS

❑ Starting to save as early as possible can make a tremendous difference in the outcome.

❑ Putting 529 plans on the list of must-haves when a child is young will serve the family well in the long run.

❑ It is possible to avoid the burden of debt and regret by opening an account and funding it regularly.

CHAPTER 17

REMAINING FULLY ALERT WHILE AT THE WHEEL: MAKING SMART MOVES AND AVOIDING WRONG TURNS BEFORE THE SPEND-DOWN PHASE OF YOUR JOURNEY BEGINS

As you come closer to reaching your destination, it is no time to take your eyes off the road for even a moment. In the years leading up to the latter part of high school, if you keep your eyes wide open, you will encounter a number of opportunities to reduce educational expenses well before your child even reaches college. There are many sensible strategies that you and your family can employ even prior to high school that will help you ultimately spend less on college, get the most out of the money you've saved, and lead your child(ren) to rewarding educational experiences and careers. In fact, author and academic strategist Jeannie Burlowski, has written an excellent book called *LAUNCH: How to Get Your Kids Through College Debt-Free and Into Jobs They Love Afterward,* in which she includes a detailed step-by-step guide for parents to use beginning in middle school to help set their child(ren) up to succeed in whatever form of post-secondary education they pursue, to graduate free of debt, and to identify fitting careers that they love and in which they will thrive. As one example of a step that can be taken in middle school, she suggests helping your child(ren) develop time management and study skills to boost confidence and productivity heading into high school and beyond.[16]

Once your child reaches high school, one of the many strategies you want to consider is arranging for your child to receive tutoring on subjects with which they are struggling and to take test preparation classes to increase the likelihood of higher scores on standardized tests. Tutoring may help your child improve grade point averages and test prep may improve standardized test scores, both of which may increase your child's chances of academic/merit scholarships. Keep in mind that there are many options for tutoring and test prep and you do not need to overspend on this. To cover these costs, if you happen to have funds in an UGMA or UTMA account, you may want to consider using those funds for various purposes that will help your child become a more highly-sought and better prepared college applicant—since those funds must be used for the benefit of your child and if unused, will count much more heavily toward your family's EFC than parental assets like 529 college savings plans (as discussed in Chapter 12).

Another approach you will want to consider is to have your child take advanced placement courses in high school that can count for college credit and thereby, lower college costs. Dual enrollment (taking college classes during high school) can be beneficial as well in acquiring credits before officially beginning college.

---

[16] Burlowski, Jeannie. *LAUNCH: How to Get Your Kids Through College Debt-Free and Into Jobs They Love Afterward.* Falcon Heights Publishing, LLC., 1st Edition, 2017.

Even before accumulating college credits in high school, have your child begin to express interest in schools as early as ninth or tenth grade to begin to show what schools refer to as a *demonstrated interest.* This can help your child get on those schools' radar screens to become top of mind for offers of admission and scholarship opportunities. Schools are often most interested in qualified students who show sincere interest in them. Your child can show interest by requesting materials or information from the schools, meeting with a school's representative(s) when they are in your area either at your child's high school or at a regional college fair, visiting the campus, participating in webinars for prospective students, following and engaging with schools on social media, and even sending a resume and statement of interest to schools well before the formal application process. When it comes time to apply, your child may wish to request an interview to more formally express interest, but even without an interview it's likely that the schools will have been tracking the number of touch points leading up to application time and will be well aware of the high level of interest.

As another strategy to reduce costs, you may want to start early researching as a family all available grant and scholarship opportunities that you can identify including anything available through your employer, community organizations, local businesses, or through activities or clubs of special interest to your child. The sooner you can identify possible sources of financial assistance and the criteria for each, the better your child will be positioned to apply and be seriously considered as a qualified candidate. For instance, if a specific grade point average or level of community engagement is required, your child will have time to prepare if you conduct research in ninth or tenth grade.

Beyond these steps, it's important at this juncture to realize that while you've come so far, you simply cannot risk becoming a distracted driver or fully stepping out of the driver's seat when it comes to considering the financial implications of the schools that are of greatest interest to your child. After diligently saving for post-secondary education, the last thing you want to do is to make an uninformed or emotionally charged decision which can lead to unfavorable financial and academic results. You'll want to exercise the same level of care you exercised with saving and investing when comparing educational options and making a final selection. Far too many students and parents select a "dream school," no matter the net cost.

What parents and students often overlook is that a dream school that is well out of reach financially can keep you from what otherwise may have been a life free of the burden associated with high levels of student loan debt. Allowing emotions to get in the way of rational decisions can cause you to spend your savings down quickly and/or carelessly or cause you or your child to wind up taking on an unnecessary amount of student loan debt. **Emotions should not drive major financial decisions, and the major investment you will make in higher education is no exception.** It will likely be one of the largest financial investments you make as a family. For an outside perspective, you may want to seek the support of an expert at this stage of your journey. As one example, nationally recognized best-selling author of *The College Solution: A Guide for Everyone Looking for the Right School at the Right Price* and other publications, Lynn O'Shaughnessy, offers valuable information through her popular blog, www.thecollegesolution.com and online course called The College Solution Cost Lab. I personally have benefitted from her expertise and perspective.

Whether or not you, as a parent, engage a third party to help facilitate good decisions in the end, you'll want to have an honest conversation about finances before, during, and after the college search. You'll want to keep in mind that the rational part of your child's brain is not fully developed until about age 25, and it is far too much responsibility to place on your child to make a decision that can have long-term consequences including adverse financial ones. It is essential that you as parent stay involved with the college decision making and funding process. Your child is simply not equipped to make a financial decision of this magnitude without the perspective of one or more adults.

If you had been talking to your child through the years about their 529 college savings account and about strategies your family was undertaking to save, the conversation will be a natural progression. It will be important to avoid getting one's heart set on a particular school. Ideally, your child and others involved in the decision process can be open-minded about options. This will provide you with an opportunity to spend smartly in the end.

School selection is critical and taking an honest look at the financial reality of various options before applications are submitted is a critical practice. Many college planning experts recommend that families place a particular focus on schools that are a good fit for the child and for the family's budget. You'll want to compare net costs and, to the extent possible, the return on investment for what your child intends to study. College planning experts also feel there is no harm in applying to one or two expensive private universities that are a good fit provided your child understands that if admitted, their ability to attend will be based on the value of the financial aid package offered and your family's ability to afford its expected financial contribution.

Other approaches include applying to schools that have "no loan" policies or, provided they have a number of strong programs that interest your child, schools that are lower ranked than those to which your child would otherwise likely be admitted. A lower-ranked college may offer your child more financial aid based on the child's academic performance—merit aid—than more highly ranked institutions.

Another approach is to consider colleges that are closer to home or in your home state to avoid having to pay out-of-state tuition as well as high transportation costs on breaks as semesters begin and end. It's important to keep in mind, however, that applying to out-of-state schools, even if perceived to be too expensive, may result in generous merit aid if the schools are trying to increase attendance by out-of-state students. You should also check with your state's higher education governing body for possible reciprocal relationships across state borders—for example in New England, the Regional Student Program provides reduced tuition costs between states at public institutions.[17]

Another strategy is to begin at a less expensive school and then transfer to a dream school after a year or two. This approach can lower overall expenses and can eventually lead to the same goal, as long as your child is committed to following through and as long as the credits already acquired can be transferred. This also allows time for the student to better understand and refine their academic and career goals. The topic of where or how their academic studies began rarely comes up once a student has their degree. As I've heard my friend and former client, Gail Mance-Rios, former Director of the Rhode Island Higher Education Assistance Authority, say, "Remember that folks don't ask 'Where did you start college?'— instead, they ask 'Where did you graduate from?'"

Additionally, some families consider a college within driving distance so that the child can live at home for one or more years to lower expenses. There are many schools that have a significant number of students who commute to and from campus each day.

Whatever approaches you choose, it's essential submit your financial aid application(s) as early as possible.

---

[17] https://nebhe.org/tuitionbreak/

As you consider the finalist schools, it's important to make certain your child is getting the maximum financial assistance available and that nothing has been misinterpreted or overlooked regarding your family's circumstances. You will want to make certain that you and your child understand exactly how the financial aid package works from the first to the last year of enrollment. For instance, you'll want to confirm that scholarship funds are divided equally over each of the years of the program in which your child is enrolling and not more heavily provided upfront, leaving you in a pickle in later years. Remember that you must apply for financial aid every year the student is an undergraduate. Additionally, if you suspect there's been a mistake or if there has been a change in your family's circumstances since initially filling out the financial aid application(s), you will want to consider appealing the first financial aid package offered.

Further, once enrolled, you will want to make certain that your child understands the importance of staying on track to graduate **on time** (or even early). The majority of students take six years or more to graduate and the additional time in school adds to the overall cost. Research options to take classes during the summer or winter breaks.

And lastly, you may want to explore with the school whether there are opportunities such as becoming a resident advisor in one of the dormitories (which could result in having the cost of room and board partially reduced), research positions, or other forms of work that may help with overall costs. These can be helpful provided the employment does not interfere with the ability to focus on academics.

College work study jobs have improved since I was in school. Many colleges try to match the work study job with the student's interests. It also makes it easier to get time off to study when you are employed by the college.

After you have all the information you need from the schools of greatest interest, and before making a final decision, you and your child should be on the same page about the extent to which your family can cover the costs. If there are not adequate funds available to cover the full cost after grants, scholarships and other forms of *free* aid are applied, you and your child will need to consider whether you are comfortable with taking student loans. You'll need to have a candid conversation about the amount that will need to be borrowed, who will be responsible for repayment and what impact that will have on life after college and for how many years.

Just as you need to keep your eyes wide open when driving, your and your child's eyes need to be particularly wide open about the reality of student loan debt. You and your child will want to discuss whether going deeply in debt for a dream school is worth it especially if the weight of student loans will cause years of repayment nightmares. You will also want to discuss whether getting the best education possible for the least amount of money will lead to a brighter and lighter future. As a rule of thumb for those who need to borrow, college funding expert Mark Kantrowitz[18] of Savingforcollege.com recommends that students borrow no more than what they will earn

---

[18] Mark Kantrowitz, Publisher and VP of Research, Savingforcollege.com

in their first-year salary.

Stories from the Road

I have met and heard from many parents and students who owe little or no educational debt and who continue to celebrate the thoughtful decisions they made about which college to attend. Often times those decisions were emotionally challenging and meant walking away from a "dream school" but in retrospect, they appreciate the fact that they still had a wonderful educational experience and can enjoy a good quality of life without tremendous debt.

The daughter of a couple I know well attended community college before transferring to a top-ranked four-year university in the city in which she lives. She took only core courses at the community college to ensure all of the credits she earned for the classes she took would be accepted by the university to which she transferred. By attending school through the summer term, she was able to finish in one-and-a-half years. She then attended a top-ranked university and finished her junior and senior years in just one-and-a-half years at a fraction of its cost. By having their daughter start at a community college, earning scholarships while there, living at home while attending college, and attending school through the summer, the couple saved enough to be able to pay in-full for their daughter to attend law school from which she graduated in 2019, totally debt free.

KEY TAKE-AWAYS

❑ Consider steps you and your child can take as early as middle school and the start of high school to begin to prepare for college and to potentially lower costs.

❑ Keep your eyes wide open at this juncture, and keep a level head as college is a tremendous investment for which you want to spend wisely.

❑ One of the surest ways to avoid additional costs is for your child to graduate on time.

❑ Your child may be able to wind up with a dream life (with little or no debt) by avoiding a dream college that your family cannot afford.

CHAPTER 18

ARRIVING SAFELY: CELEBRATING YOUR CONTRIBUTION AS YOU EMBRACE THE OPEN ROAD AHEAD OF THEM

Cue the confetti. At last, your future self will have arrived at the moment you've long been preparing for and congratulations will be in order! Your child will be heading off to college or career training and you will be well-prepared for this leg of the trip.

With your car fully packed as you begin your journey to college drop off day, you'll look through your windshield with excitement at the wide-open road ahead and all the possibilities that await your child. And you will very likely take a well-deserved moment to glance in the rearview mirror to look back with pride at the consistent steps you undertook over the years to get where you now are. Perhaps you'll even remember that your journey began by reading this book. In the years that follow, you'll continue to celebrate the sense of achievement that comes with having planned ahead.

A Peek into My Journey

Now that his college years are upon us, I cannot tell you the sense of relief associated with being well-prepared for our son's education after high school. Having diligently contributed to his accounts over 18 years, we have both peace of mind and the options we had hoped for. Saving in advance provided flexibility in our son's choice of schools, choice of major, other experiences including study abroad options, and his ability to take unpaid summer internship roles that were of particular interest to him.

The future we had envisioned when we started on our savings journey when our son was an infant has now been fully realized. We wanted him to have a less financially stressful academic experience than we had as students and we wanted to help him avoid the weight of student loan debt that we carried with us for nearly twenty years following the attainment of our degrees.

I believe firmly that you too can realize the vision you have for your child(ren)'s future. Travel safely and savor your journey.

"You have the ability to change or create anything in your life, starting now."

~Hal Elrod, *The Miracle Morning*[19]

---

[19] Elrod, Hal. *The Miracle Morning: The Not-so-obvious Secret Guaranteed to Transform Your Life Before 8AM.* Hal Elrod International, 2014.

Appendix

5 STEPS TO KEEP YOU **ON TRACK**

☐ Keep your **WHY** top of mind.

☐ Continue to make automatic contributions and increase them over time. Sign up for payroll deduction if your employer permits.

☐ Cut expenses, invest those savings and deposit extra money (from tax refunds, salary increases, graduating out of diapers or daycare, etc.) into your college savings account.

☐ Continue to invite friends, family and your employer to contribute and get your children involved as they grow older.

☐ Conduct an annual (or more frequent) check-up on your own, or with an advisor if you have one, to examine your progress toward your goal. Consider any adjustments that need to be made to help you to reach your destination and keep in mind any changes in your time horizon, risk tolerance or objectives.

STATES WITH DEDUCTIONS OR CREDITS FOR 529 COLLEGE SAVINGS PLAN CONTRIBUTIONS

Tax Credit or Deduction (Single Filer/Joint Filers)

Alabama	Deduction up to $5,000/$10,000
Arizona[1]	Deduction up to $2,000/$4,000
Arkansas[1,2]	Deduction up to $5,000/$10,000 for AR 529. For out of state plans, there is a reduced deduction of $3,000/$6,000
Colorado	Deduction of full contribution amount up to contributor's taxable income
Connecticut[2]	Deduction up to $5,000/$10,000
D.C.[2]	Deduction up to $4,000/$8,000
Georgia	Deduction up to $4,000/$8,000 per beneficiary
Idaho	Deduction up to $6,000/$12,000
Illinois	Deduction up to $10,000/$20,000
Indiana	20% tax credit on contributions of up to $5,000; max. credit is $1,000
Iowa	Deduction of up to $3,439/$6,878 per beneficiary (Note: This is the 2020 amount and is subject to annual adjustment for inflation.)
Kansas[1]	Deduction up to $3,000/$6,000 per beneficiary
Louisiana[2]	Deduction up to $2,400/$4,800 per beneficiary
Maryland[2]	Deduction up to $2,500/$5,000 per beneficiary
Massachusetts	$1,000/$2,000 deduction (This is currently effective through tax year 2021.)
Michigan	Deduction up to $5,000/$10,000
Minnesota[1]	Deduction up to $1,500/$3,000 or non-refundable tax credit of up to $500 subject to various conditions
Mississippi	Deduction up to $10,000/$20,000
Missouri[1]	Deduction up to $8,000/$16,000

Montana[1]	Deduction up to $3,000/$6,000
Nebraska	Deduction up to $10,000 per tax return (or $5,000 for married taxpayers filing separate returns)
New Mexico	Deduction of full contribution amount
New York	Deduction up to $5,000/$10,000
North Dakota	Deduction up to $5,000/$10,000
Ohio[2]	Deduction up to $4,000/$4,000 per beneficiary
Oklahoma[2]	Deduction up to $10,000/$20,000
Oregon[2]	Up to $150 tax credit for single filers and up to $300 tax credit for joint filers. (The amount the taxpayer must contribute to get the full credit increases based on the taxpayer's income. May be adjusted annually. Currently scheduled to expire on 1/1/2026.)
Pennsylvania[1]	Deduction up to $15,000/$30,000 per beneficiary
Rhode Island[2]	Deduction up to $500/$1,000
South Carolina	Deduction of full contribution amount
Utah	5% tax credit on contributions up to $2,040/$4,080 with a max. credit of $102/$204 per beneficiary. (This is the 2020 amount and is subject to annual adjustment for inflation.)
Vermont	10% tax credit on contributions up to $2,500 / $5000) with a max credit of $250/$500 per beneficiary
Virginia[2]	Deduction up to $4,000 per account and fully deductible if 70 or older
West Virginia[2]	Deduction of full contribution amount
Wisconsin[2]	Deduction up to $3,340 per beneficiary. (This is the 2020 amount and is subject to annual adjustment for inflation.)

Tax treatment listed above is believed to be accurate as of publication but is subject to change. Check the details of your state's tax treatment carefully to determine who can take a deduction or credit and whether there are special conditions such as recapture.

[1]Taxpayers in AR, AZ, KS, MN, MO, MT and PA may be eligible for a state tax benefit whether they invest in their home state 529 college savings plan or any other 529 college savings plan.

[2]Taxpayers in AR, CT, DC, LA, MD, OH, OK, OR, RI, VA, WI and WV may carry forward excess contributions to subsequent tax years. Check your state for specific details.

ADDITIONAL RESOURCES

Here are additional resources about planning for college and college costs that I have utilized which may also be useful to you:

Burlowski, Jeannie. *LAUNCH: How to Get Your Kids Through College Debt-Free and Into Jobs They Love Afterward.* Falcon Heights Publishing, LLC. 1st Edition, December 2017.

Hupalo, John A. and Peter Mazareas, Ph.D. *Plan and Finance Your Family's College Dreams.* Peterson's, 1st Edition, May 2016.

Hurley, Joseph, et. al. *The Best Way to Save for College: A Complete Guide to 529 Plans.* Savingforcollege.com Publications, 12th edition, August 2018.

O'Shaughnessy, Lynn. *The College Solution: A Guide for Everyone Looking for the Right School at the Right Price.* FT Press, 2nd Edition, May 2012.

529 Plan Comparison Tools and Information:

www.Savingforcollege.com

The College Savings Plans Network

www.collegesavings.org

Other Resources:

www.mycollegecorner.com

www.thecollegesolution.com

The College Savings Foundation

www.collegesavingsfoundation.org

National Center for Education Statistics College Navigator

www.nces.ed.gov/collegenavigator/

Federal Student Aid (an Office of the U.S. Department of Education)

www.studentaid.gov/h/understand-aid

529A (ABLE) Plan Information:

The National Association of State Treasurers

www.nast.org/able

ABLE National Resource Center

www.ablenrc.org

ACKNOWLEDGMENTS

Many thanks are owed to the following individuals who offered both their subject matter expertise and valuable perspective in the review of this book: Susie Bauer, Young Boozer, Beth Bordowitz, Margaret Clancy, Betty Lochner, and Gail Mance-Rios.

Thank you as well to Eric Bennett and the Bennett Collaborative for editing support, to Rick Roberts and Michael Sheu for analytic support, to Nadia Standard/standardesign for support on the visuals within the book, and Krista Dunk of Author Acceleration Academy for publishing support.

Many thanks to Mel Robbins whose *Power of You* coaching awakened in me my desire to write this book. Heartfelt thanks as well to Hal Elrod whose *Miracle Morning* helps me start each day with a positive and productive mindset. And thanks to Joshua Becker who helped me to find greater clarity and peace by embracing a minimalist lifestyle. A book like this does not come to be without purpose and passion—and a pandemic, which provided me with a bit of extra time to put it together.

To my family and friends, I thank each of you for your ongoing encouragement and enthusiasm for my work. A tremendous amount of appreciation is owed to Anthony, for together raising such a wonderful son and for sharing in the commitment to save for his future. And to Ben, not only for the beautiful foreword you wrote and the cover you helped design, but for the inspiration you provide every day. Your dad and I are so very proud of you.

And lastly, to each of the families I've personally met and have learned of along the way while working with 529 college savings plans. While your stories differ in various ways, your love for the children in your life and your desire to provide bright futures for them are very much the same. I am inspired by your determination to make a positive impact. It is for you that I and countless others across the nation have tirelessly worked over the past few decades to raise awareness of the existence and usefulness of 529 plans and to make them as accessible as possible. We celebrate you and the children you love and will continue to work hard to help make your educational goals attainable.

Photo credit (back cover): Lucas Fenton

Author Biography

A life-long learner with a deep appreciation for the many doors higher education can open, **Patricia Roberts** has helped tens of thousands of families prepare for the cost of higher education through her leadership in nearly every aspect of the 529 college savings arena over the past 20 years.

She is currently Chief Operating Officer at Gift of College, Inc., which offers an innovative crowdfunding platform to enable friends, family and employers to contribute to others' 529 college savings, ABLE and student loan accounts, and which offers gift cards online and in major retailers that can be contributed to these accounts as well. She is particularly focused on bringing awareness of 529 plans to the workplace as a voluntary benefit so that many more Americans can become acquainted with these plans and begin using them to plan for the future and to avoid or minimize the need for student loan debt.

Prior to this, she held key legal, product, and 529 program management roles at major financial services firms and she designed and launched several first-of-their-kind philanthropic programs through which families received seed money for college savings accounts along with valuable financial education and incentives to help them save on their own.

As a motivational speaker and writer, she is interested in inspiring and empowering all families to have better outcomes by planning ahead for financial goals. She has a particular interest in those that may have a more challenging time getting and staying on track, including families with lower incomes, those in which no one has yet pursued higher education, and families with students who have special needs. Since the creation of 529A (ABLE) plans in 2014, she has worked with the disability community to raise awareness of the existence and usefulness of these plans as well.

Having financed her own undergraduate and law degrees while working multiple jobs and having repaid sizable student loans as a first-generation college goer, she knows first-hand the difference that even a small amount of advanced planning can make in paying for higher education and in helping students stay focused on completing their education.

In her favorite role of all, she made it a priority to save a little at a time for her son's higher education expenses by directing contributions from her paycheck into 529 college savings accounts. After 18 years of saving, she will be proud to see him graduate debt-free from college in 2021.

Patricia holds a B.A. in Philosophy and Political Science from Duquesne University and a J.D. from Brooklyn Law School.

INDEX

CONTINUED LEARNING

Visit www.Route529.com

To request a presentation, workshop, or interview, contact:
info@route529.com

Presentation/discussion topics include:

- 529 Plan Basics: What Every Parent & Grandparent Needs to Know
- The Value of 529 Plans in the Workplace
- Myth Busting: The Truth about 529 College Savings Plans
- ABLE Plan Basics
- Addressing the Student Loan Crisis with 529 Plans
- Getting from Where You Are to Where You Want to Be: Strategies for Success
- Rallying Friends & Family to Join You on Your Savings Journey
- Small Steps to Big Change
- Financial Literacy Starts at Home